WHERE THE GODS DWELL

WHERE THE GODS DWELL

THIRTEEN TEMPLES AND THEIR (HI)STORIES

Edited by
Karthik Venkatesh

WESTLAND
NON·FICTION

WESTLAND
NON·FICTION

First published by Westland Non-Fiction, an imprint of Westland Publications Private Limited, in 2021

Published by Westland Non-Fiction, an imprint of Westland Books, a division of Nasadiya Technologies Private Limited, in 2025

Westland, the Westland logo, Westland Non-Fiction and the Westland Non-Fiction logo are the trademarks of Nasadiya Technologies Private Limited, or its affiliates.

ISBN: 9789371977074

10 9 8 7 6 5 4 3 2 1

The views and opinions expressed in these essays are the authors' own and the facts are as reported by them, and the publisher is in no way liable for the same.

Typeset by SÜRYA, New Delhi

Printed at Nutech Print Services, India

Contents

The (Hi)story of the Book's Making

The idea for this book germinated in a conversation. A friend recounted the story of a temple that he had recently visited. The narrative contained a fair amount of historical elements besides being a lovely excursion into some very fascinating mythology. This prompted another to share a similar-sounding story of a temple that she had visited. While there were some commonalities between the stories, the accounts were also markedly different, both in their historical as well as mythological details.

As the story-telling session moved on to include others, the idea for the book began to appear obvious. It would be, we thought, fascinating to commission essays by writers on the stories of temples from different parts of the country, perhaps even the subcontinent. The stories, one suspected, would be a combination of history and mythology. They would be both a historical journey and feature a generous dollop of mythology, which, in most cases, would almost certainly contain a local twist.

Writers were identified, lists of temples drawn up and e-mails sent. The response was tremendous. Virtually everyone we wrote to, agreed to contribute. Some of them even had suggestions about which temples we should feature, prompting a rethink of some of the original temples on the list. Over a few months, through a process of elimination and suggestion, the final list came to be.

When it came to the title, the first half of the title (*Where the Gods Dwell*) suggested itself almost organically. For the second half (the subtitle: *Thirteen Temples and their (Hi)stories*), some meditation was required to hit upon the right word that would, in a flash, capture the essence of the essays. Hence the term '(hi)story'. Virtually, all the essays dive deep into history and mythology. Given that, '(hi)story' which stressed on both the historical and mythological aspects of the writings seemed a better choice than just 'history' or 'story'. The (hi)stories, in most instances, also include an architectural discussion of the temples.

Manu Pillai's essay talks of the fabled Padmanabhaswami temple of Thiruvananthapuram which has been in the news over the last few years for the treasures it supposedly holds in its vaults. The real treasure though is the fascinating (hi)story of the temple, recounted by Manu in his own inimitable style. Basav Biradar's account of the Virupaksha temple at Hampi is an interesting take encompassing history and mythology, of course, but also, issues arising out of the fact that Hampi is a fabled tourist destination.

Indira Vishwanathan Peterson's (hi)story of the Brihadisvara temple in Tanjore and Meera Iyer's of the temples of Belur and Halebidu feature some very absorbing discussions of temple architecture. Shrenik Rao's essay on the Rudreswara temple gives interesting insights into the historical background that prompted the building of the temple. This temple is the most recent addition to the UNESCO world heritage list, having earned the honour in July 2021, just as we were going to press.

Siddhartha Sarma's essay offers a comprehensive view of the Kamakhya temple in Assam, delineating the temple's uniqueness and a rounded account of its rituals and practices. Neelesh Kulkarni's long association with the Pandharpur temple has provided him a unique view of the temple's journey over the last few decades. Vikrant Pande's journey to Somnath while presenting the history and mythology also delves into its recent history and attempts to contextualise it. Contextualisation is also something that is evident in Trisha Gupta's essay on Khajuraho. Both Vikrant's and Trisha's essays also feature riveting discussions that the authors had with an omnipresent entity in most important temples (indeed, most important monuments) in India—the tour guide. Approaching the art and the craft of the guide from different angles, these essays introduce yet another element to the anthology.

The anthology also features essays on the Pashupatinath temple in Nepal (by Amish Raj Mulmi), the Katas Raj temple in Pakistan (by Haroon Khalid) and the Nallur Kandaswamy temple in Sri Lanka (by Thulasi Muttulingam). Their blend of mythology and history, coupled with their location in a different country, ensures that the similarities and their differences can be seen in the light of the unique conditions that prevail in each country.

Siddhartha Gigoo's essay that features a temple in Srinagar that was part of his growing-up years in the Valley is a personal story and a personal history. Poignant yet pragmatic, it offers a different perspective.

Needless to say, this book is the product of a list that was drawn up by a few people. Could some more temples have been added to the list? Of course. But given the exigencies of space and the plan to have an accessibly priced volume, many had to be left out. Have some 'important' temples been left out? Very likely. The difficulties of finding a writer who would be able to commit to such a project and deliver in time prompted some temples to be left out of the list. Yet, the list of temples that features in the anthology is a fascinating one and the book promises hours of reading pleasure besides a generous helping of history and mythology, or to put it better, (hi)story!

The God Who Ate from a Coconut Shell

Manu S. Pillai

In the mid-nineteenth century, there was a maharajah in Travancore who was a man of great originality. Though in his kingly avatar he was hesitant to challenge antiquated customs, as an individual he was unorthodox. He sat for portraits in Western coat and trousers and watched Englishmen down meaty, 'impure' dinners. An amateur doctor and chemist, he loved the idea of modern science, having his craftsmen build him a skeleton of ivory so he could study anatomy undefiled by human bones. Even as he spent astronomical sums on grand old Brahminical rites, he did not hesitate to ensure his children learnt English, with Christian scripture for textbooks. But if the maharajah was a social success in colonial circles, as a *ruler* his political record was less unblemished. Reports circulated of outrageous abuses in his government, and, worryingly for his British bosses, of Travancore's finances being in the red. Less than a decade into his reign, then, a 'most dreadful' communique arrived at the palace, warning the man to mend his ways.[1] And at the top of the list was an urgent need to balance his accounts and pay off his arrears—or prepare for ominous talk of annexation and intervention from upstairs.

'The descent of this thunderbolt', his nephew would write, created an 'immense stir'. While reining in corruption and improving efficiency were doable with a new crop of assistants, where was money to be found to stave off immediate pressure? In his hour of need, therefore, the maharajah turned to his deity—and not for spiritual consolation alone. The Padmanabhaswami temple, dynastic shrine to Travancore's kings, was a splendidly wealthy institution, even if in appearance it pales before the great shrines of neighbouring Tamil provinces. It owned tens of thousands of acres of agricultural real estate, besides a hoard of treasure, maintaining all along a handsome liquid fund for contingencies. While in theory these were the deity's goods, with the state in dire need, the royal application for help was received sympathetically. And so, half a million rupees were loaned to our kingly supplicant, at an interest rate of five per cent.[2] Or as the maharajah's nephew put its less delicately: 'The ancient vaults of the great Pagoda were ransacked, and five lakhs of rupees scraped out', so that over the next few years the eye of the white man in British Madras could be warded off this southern principality.[3]

That Padmanabhaswami saved Travancore from the British in the 1850s is not surprising, given how the deity had helped in the very making of the state a century before. In fact, to visit the temple is to straddle several ages. There are cameras and glimpses of ugly wiring to remind us of our own world today, while grand old structures tell stories from many yesterdays. There is the seven-storied gopuram, a hundred feet high, with stucco and brick sculptures featuring Vishnu's incarnations and puranic figures. There are gilded pillars and magnificent corridors, held up by carved granite: the work of a proverbial ten thousand hands and a hundred elephants. There are mural paintings of great charm and beauty, and shrines to minor gods with their own mythologies. There is the ottakkal mandapam, carved from a single rock that took forty-two days and men from a dozen villages to drag from a nearby hill.[4] And then there are the anecdotes that circulate: one narrates that with all the hacking and sculpting while making these eighteenth-century structures, granite chips were strewn around the seven-acre premises. The clean-up was so slow, that the king himself carried a load—at once, all those watching joined in, and the place was cleared up in no time.[5] For in the presence of the divine, even the sovereign was a servant.

The Padmanabhaswami temple's present-day incarnation, in fact, is tied specifically to the life of this load-bearing king, Martanda Varma (reigned 1729–58). Once upon a time, the complex wore a simpler look, like most Kerala temples: the principal entrance was not a Tamil-style stone gopuram, but followed the padippura design familiar to Malayalis, with gables and a thatched roof. The great corridor with its 365 pillars did not exist—why, even the image of the deity was made of wood, and not with the 12,008 sacred saligrama stones that we behold today. It was in the fourteenth century that an ancestor of the Travancore maharajahs gave the place a splash of glamour through a reconstruction. But this again—in consonance with the Kerala style—elevated delicate woodwork and carpentry, not stately stone and granite as preferred 400 years later.[6] Most of its results were lost, however, in 1686: a fire devoured the temple, burning even the roof of the sanctum. Precious metals and gems stored there burst onto the ground, while the deity's idol was scorched, losing fingers and toes.[7] The kings who reigned thereafter—rulers of a tiny kingdom with limited means—could only make modest repairs, and it fell on

Martanda Varma to rebuild Padmanabhaswami's abode, giving it a fresh, enduring air of grandeur.

This maharajah's official narrative—one which weds dynasty to deity with an umbilical bond—is interesting. The Sanskrit *Balamartandavijaya* begins with the young Martanda Varma recalling a vision he has had. He was commanded, he tells his minister, by Padmanabhaswami himself to renovate his shrine, which had languished for too long in gloomy disrepair. But because the mission entailed a massive outflow of funds, and as the deity knew that Martanda Varma could barely make ends meet, the king was granted heavenly sanction to subdue other princes; he was to seize their territories and place their wealth at his patron god's disposal.[8] And that is precisely what he did: he marched out, vanquished his neighbours, and returning with their riches, not only gave the deity a befitting home, but also dedicated his conquests to the lord, ruling thereafter as regent. Indeed, when construction was finished for most part, and the new image ready for consecration in the sanctum,[9] it was Martanda Varma himself who affixed the gold finials atop its vimana.[10] And as is well known today, ever since 1750, after a rite called trippadidanam, the kings of Travancore ruled their country as Padmanabha Dasas—servants of god—a title worn so seriously that after Independence, the last maharajah was hesitant to take an oath as head of state, because he did not believe he was its head in the first place.[11]

That said, while the *Balamartandavijaya* amplifies royal connections with the temple, the site in its own right has legends that predate all kings. Though orthodox tradition places the temple's consecration on the 'first day of the Kali Yuga' (the last of four Hindu time cycles), giving it a 5,000-year provenance,[12] historians have settled on the eighth and ninth centuries CE as the more reasonable date for the event. Several major shrines in Kerala belong to this period—such as the great Siva temple at Kandiyur—and a reference in the verses of the contemporary Vaishnava saint Nammalvar evidently praises this temple in Thiruvananthapuram. But even the traditionalists have more than one origin myth, depending on who, and of what class and caste, is narrating the story. Indeed, the two most popular versions repeated today feature Brahmins as founders of the shrine, while a third, barely mentioned now, ascribes that honour not to a high-caste man but a Dalit woman, and *her* encounter with the divine.[13] As with most legends and oral narratives, though, echoes of truth exist in all versions. These, when read together, help reconstruct the evolution of a local house of worship, venerated by the smallfolk, into a major institution that later shaped Travancore's kingship.

The Brahmin stories follow the same pattern, but with different protagonists: in one, it is a saint called Divakara Muni, while in the other it is Vilvamangalam Swamiyar, linked with multiple temples in Kerala. The broad arc is as follows: the saint, a devotee of Vishnu, was engaged in intense meditation, when a little boy would, seemingly out of nowhere, appear and disturb him. In one instance, the protagonist, eyes shut, smacks the boy with his hand, while in another, when the child picks up the man's saligrama and irreverently puts it in his mouth, he is given a serious dressing down. In both cases, the boy vanishes with the words, 'If you wish to see me again, you can find me in Ananthankadu.' Realising that the mischievous disruptor was none other than Vishnu himself, the saint wanders in search of the place mentioned. In one version, the man gets there himself, and sees the boy disappear into the hollow of an illupa tree, while in the other, he passes a Pulaya woman, and hearing her berate an irritating infant—'If you keep crying I'll throw you into Ananthankadu!'—has her show him the way. Either way, the tree crashes down soon enough, and Vishnu appears in ananthasayanam, as Padmanabhaswami.[14] Indeed, we are told, it was with the wood of the same illupa that the original image of the deity was constructed, to which pooja was done till Martanda Varma installed the present one.[15]

Interestingly, however, the third legend does not feature Brahmins, or even Vishnu as such. In it we hear of a Pulaya woman—whose community, despite legends of their own kings, was reduced to agrestic slavery and are today a scheduled caste—is tilling her field when she comes across a baby. Sensing something special in the child, she washes herself, feeds it from her breast, and leaves it under the shade of a tree (presumably illupa) to resume work. On her return, she finds a five-headed cobra shielding the child in the hollow of that tree. Convinced that the baby is divine, the Pulaya lady and her husband begin worship on the spot. In time, the place's reputation grew, and a full-fledged temple sprang up, transforming a kadu (forest) into a sacred town.[16] This local, possibly tribal origin of the deity, later merged with Vishnu of the Sanskritic 'Great Tradition', continues to find resonance in ritual practices to this day. Indeed, all three origin myths cast their protagonists as presenting naivedyam (offering) to the deity—of rice gruel and raw mangoes—in a coconut shell, and even the Brahmin sthalapuranas (local histories) do not deny the temple's humble beginnings.[17] And while the Pulaya story is generally footnoted now, Padmanabhaswami continues to be served in a coconut shell, albeit covered with gold foil. After all, he is no longer a forest god but one of the world's wealthiest divinities.

As it happens, these rival origin myths offer tantalising clues as to the evolution of Brahminical Hinduism in the region. For instance, Divakara Muni is said to have been a Tulu Brahmin; even now, the principal priestly families associated with the Padmanabhaswami temple are Potties of Tulu origin.[18] Vilvamangalam Swamiyar, on the other hand, was a Namboothiri, and to this day, the head tantri (priest) at the shrine is from this community.[19] Could it be that these tales allude to Brahmin immigration into a non-Brahmin cultural zone? After all, Kerala's founding legend tells of the mythical Parasurama creating the land and bringing in twice-born occupants; the journey of the two saints from up the coast to Ananthankadu near the southern tip offers a parallel, just as the Pulaya legend suggests a non-Sanskritic origin to the shrine. It would not be terribly surprising: it is acknowledged now that the Sabarimala temple was once under tribal ownership, for example, before its deity was Sanskritised. Reinventing holy sites linked with other groups extended even to faiths not bracketed as Hindu—the discovery of an image of the Buddha from a field near the Kandiyur Siva temple, thus, has birthed speculation as to its pre-Brahmin history.[20] It is within the realm of reason, then, that a tribal grove, once managed by today's marginalised castes, passed into Brahmin and princely hands, just as the jungle became a town and then a royal capital.

This last—the transformation of the Padmanabhaswami temple into a kingly shrine—was not as seamless as one would imagine, however. In the over two million palm-leaf documents that record the institution's history from the fourteenth century, local rulers are not always presented in a flattering light. Of course, there are records of grand donations: of kings granting large sums of money, valuables such as gold and silver ornaments, landed estates, and much else, just as there is evidence of private individuals also demonstrating piety via the pocket.[21] But the power of the ruler over the temple was not absolute: there was a council of Brahmins (the Sabha) to attend to ritual matters, and a larger council featuring other stakeholders (the Ettarayogam) involved in the management of the temple's economic portfolio. While generally it is said that the king had half a vote on the second council, there are scholars who argue that the ruler had no place at all, and could not even sit before the yogam.[22] Whatever the truth, it is clear is that as the temple, with its landed properties and network of tenants, soldiers, and even feudal lords, grew in influence, the king's fiats were resisted. Who had how much strength depended greatly on shifting balances: sometimes the temple Brahmins would feud with their own non-Brahmin colleagues, allowing the ruler to manipulate the situation; other occasions saw royal troops clash with the sacerdotal authorities, resulting in bloody violence.

Thus, for instance, in the early seventeenth century, when one of Martanda Varma's forebears asked for certain festivals to be resumed after years of non-performance, the priests asked him to first return temple lands he had occupied 'illegally', and to agree to this in writing.[23] In the fifteenth century, the king's men prevented temple tenants from cultivating its lands, resulting in several deaths—in the end the ruler had to donate an elephant to expiate his sin.[24] Not long afterwards, in another struggle, royal troops burned the north gate of the shrine, while a third episode some years later saw twelve Brahmins wounded. As usual, when a compromise was reached, the king made expensive donations—this time of twelve silver pots—and got away with his deeds.[25] This is not to suggest that the temple authorities were innocent always: in the seventeenth century, valuables routinely disappeared, and it sometimes took a strong queen like Umayamma (reigned 1677–84) to restore discipline to the shrine's affairs.[26] In a sense, royal legitimacy and power depended on exercising the right to regulate temple affairs, just as its trustees saw preserving autonomy as imperative to checking kingly autocracy.

With Martanda Varma, however, this old system perished. Historically speaking, when he came to power, there was no Travancore. A sliver of the coast between Thiruvananthapuram and Kanyakumari was ruled by the Venad family, while relatives controlled other patches. The grandest coastal kingdom was still that of the Zamorin of Calicut (in whose court Vasco da Gama landed), while within Venad, power was widely dispersed among regional satraps and institutions. As one prince complained, 'The nobles only desire that the kings sit on the throne like mute statues and do only what the nobles wish them to do.'[27] Martanda Varma, however, set himself against this system of shared power, and even before succession urged centralisation. Naturally, he made enemies—and dramatic stories exist of foiled assassination plots—but eventually triumphed. The most bothersome nobles were liquidated, his relations' territories captured, and marching troops north, Martanda Varma defeated even the Zamorin. By the time he died, in 1758, his new state—Travancore—was Kerala's greatest, its ascent matched by the growing clout and physical glory of Padmanabhaswami. And the temple's management too was transformed: by destroying powerful nobles who controlled its estates, emasculating the Brahmin trustees, and acquiring hitherto unprecedented wealth and armed strength through his conquests, the Padmanabhaswami temple became a fully royally governed shrine.

In thus seeking absolute charge, Martanda Varma may have been motivated by devotion, but separating statecraft from the equation is difficult. For instance, during his takeover of neighbouring states, the maharajah had no qualms plundering and burning other temples.[28] This was not iconoclasm as much as a method by which the legitimacy of rival kings—who were responsible for these victimised shrines—could be smashed. But while it got the man what he wanted in terms of power, in most places he was seen as a ruthless invader. For the fact was that he destroyed noble families, displaced and banished princes who came from lines as old as his, and otherwise tormented his enemies. On conquering one state, for example, he extorted large sums from its leading residents, while forcing 15,000 others to labour on fortification projects designed to cement his grip.[29] Indeed, it is very likely that a great portion of the treasure deposited in the vaults of the Padmanabhaswami temple—which has animated people around the world following a recent effort to quantify the hoard—was originally war booty. Martanda Varma, after all, delighted in seizing the state jewels of his enemies, and it is likely that on his triumphant return from each campaign, the most valuable items were 'donated' to the deity.[30] In doing so, he had not only a material incentive, but also an occasion to flaunt kingly piety.

Demonstrating religiosity, as it happens, was essential to kingship—particularly to kings who lacked legitimacy. In many of freshly forged Travancore's districts, Martanda Varma was a recent conqueror; memories of the old kings were strong and could not be easily uprooted by armies and force. The people resisted, and it was precisely to transcend this crisis of legitimacy that the maharajah elevated Padmanabhaswami as the 'true' master of his kingdom. As the eulogistic *Balamartandvijaya* argues, he became a conqueror not to augment his power but in obedience of god; and as the trippadidanam, through which the kingdom was 'surrendered' to the deity, signalled, the new regime was not centred on a mortal, but on the almighty. Some of the Padmanabhaswami temple's iconic festivals—the Lakshadeepam with its 100,000 lamps, the sexennial Murajapam, where Brahmins from across Kerala are invited to recite the Vedas and sent home with generous gifts—were all inaugurated in this period to woo powerful classes into recognising Travancore. Of course, dynastic security for Martanda Varma's line was not neglected either. As Padmanabha Dasas, each king's actions were an earthly manifestation of divine will. Or as a court chronicler admitted, even to speak ill of the maharajah was now 'Swamy-drohum' or 'doing mischief' to the deity,[31] and the position of the ruler became akin to 'that of the Pope in Rome'—political but encased in the sacred.[32]

It was in this context too that the temple complex was renovated and the grand structures we see today erected—no one could be left in doubt that this was one of the greatest shrines in the land.[33] As for the ruling dynasty, it became difficult to separate them from Padmanabhaswami. In the colonial period, in fact, when much hard power was constrained by the British, successive rulers were able to reinvent their sovereignty, emphasising the devotional and religious element, instead of the military and political.[34] Thus, an early nineteenth century ruler, Swathi Tirunal (reigned 1829–46), boxed in and bullied by the British, found consolation in cultural areas of kingship, patronising poets, artists, and making grand donations to the temple.[35] Even the anglophile maharajah Uthram Tirunal (reigned 1846–60) mentioned in the opening part of this essay spent generously on his deity: the reverence his family commanded was a reflection, after all, of their role as Padmanabhaswami's 'servants'. Martanda Varma had recognised the value of this well in advance. On his deathbed, among the commandments he left for his heirs was that 'no deviation whatever should be made in regard to the dedication of the kingdom' to the deity.[36] The formula worked excellently, for after Independence and the dissolution of Travancore too, the royal family retained rights over the temple, benefitting from the public esteem this inspired, even when the region went under Communist rule.

In the end, it took till the twenty-first century for Martanda Varma's heirs' primacy in temple affairs to be legally challenged. Secular and judicial officials got involved, accounts books were scrutinised, and unflattering reports hinting at mismanagement filed, with even the global press taking an interest in the proceedings. Finally, in 2020, the Indian Supreme Court upheld the principle that Padmanabhaswami must always have a Padmanabha Dasa, though it was not an absolute victory for the ex-royal house. Time, after all, weathers everything, and if Martanda Varma displaced the temple councils, making the monarch its sole comptroller, matters now swung back to a system of shared management. The sheer wealth in the shrine's vaults—with some ascribing fabulous monetary values to priceless artefacts—meant that, by twenty-first century norms, a single family could not be left unsupervised, without checks and balances. Though at first, the ex-royals claimed that the temple was 'private', this position was revised to admit that it was a 'public' institution. And while the head of the Travancore house retains the right to approve extraordinary expenses, physical alterations and changes in ritual, routine administration has been devolved to a committee—or a modern-day yogam—featuring government appointees, the head priest and others.[37]

Viewed another way, though, this is merely the latest bend in a 1,000-year-old journey for Padmanabhaswami. From his days receiving simple naivedyams from a Dalit woman's hands, to owning veritable mountains of diamonds, thanks to royal patrons, the deity who reclines in the sanctum, with his consorts and other gods represented around him, is still watching the ages pass. How he is perceived, and what stories are told of him vary, but at its core there is an idea that has remained constant in its tremendous appeal. After all, that is the beauty of a great temple: no matter what vicissitudes upset the transient calculations of men, the image within is a powerful symbol, encapsulating in fascinating ways social and cultural histories. In that sense, Padmanabhaswami is not defined by his gem-studded idol or even the handsome temple complex—he is a fabric of lore and memory, one that is far more valuable than his treasures and jewels combined.

Notes

1 Quote from the maharajah's letter dated 30/12/1855 to C.F. Kohlhoff from the papers of Maharani Sethu Lakshmi Bayi of Travancore, courtesy of Dr Lakshmi Raghunandan.

2 P. Shungoonny Menon, *History of Travancore from the Earliest Times* (New Delhi: Asian Educational Services, 1998, first ed. 1878), pp. 486–87.

3 Visakham Tirunal Rama Varma in 'A Native Statesman',

p. 235 in *The Calcutta Review*, Vol. LV (Calcutta: Thomas S. Smith, 1872), pp. 225–63.

4 A.P. Ibrahim Kunju, 'The Administration of Travancore in the Eighteenth Century', p. 440 in *Journal of Kerala Studies*, Vol. 2, Part 3 (1975), pp. 425–48.

5 Ibid.

6 A. Gopalakrishna Menon, *History of Sri Padmanabaswami Temple Till 1758* (Thiruvananthapuram: Menon & Co., 1996), p. 113.

7 Ibid. p. 212.

8 See K. Sambasiva Sastri ed., *Balamartandavijayam Devarajakavivirchitam* (Devaraja Kavi's Balamartandavijaya) (Trivandrum: Government Press, 1930). See also A.G. Menon, p. 214.

9 The construction was completed well after Martanda Varma's day. The gopuram, for example, was finished by his immediate successor, while the gold finials on the gopuram's peak were only added in the 1870s, in the time of a minister called Sir Seshiah Sastri.

10 A.G. Menon, p. 217.

11 V.P. Menon, *The Story of the Integration of the Indian States* (Bombay: Orient Longmans Ltd, 1956), p. 280. He was required as head of state to take an oath to the Constitution and confirm Travancore's merger with the Indian Union in 1949.

12 See, for instance, the temple's official website at https://spst.in/golden-grace-grandeur/ (accessed 24/02/21).

13 The first two appear, thus, on the temple website (see https://spst.in/temple-history/) while the third is not mentioned at all, though as late as the early twentieth century, it was in circulation.

14 The story goes that the original form was so gigantic that the deity's head was in Thiruvallam, his middle in Thiruvananthapuram, and his feet in Thrippapur. At the

saint's request, then, Vishnu shrank himself into a more manageable size.

15 See both stories in M.S. Ramesh, *108 Vaishnavite Divya Desams: Volume Seven, Divya Desams in Malai Nadu and Vada Nadu* (Tirupati: I.V. Subba Rao, 2000), pp. 135–38.

16 V. Nagam Aiya, *The Travancore State Manual*, Vol. 2 (Trivandrum: Travancore Government Press, 1906), p. 82.

17 Ramesh, p. 136.

18 The six families are Kupakara, Vanchiyoor Atiyara, Kollur Atiyara, Neytasseri, Muttavila and Karuva.

19 Reference is to the Tarananallur Namboothiri.

20 This Buddha now sits as a public artefact at a junction in the nearby town of Mavelikara.

21 See, for instance, A.G. Menon, p. 94, where he describes one individual donating land, a bell, a lampstand, a cooking vessel and so on.

22 A.G. Menon, p. 124. See also p. 232 where he discusses other opinions on the subject of the king's authority in the temple.

23 Ibid. p. 26.

24 Ibid. p. 122.

25 Ibid. pp. 128, 138. The *Travancore State Manuals* also discuss these expiatory actions by rulers.

26 Ibid. p. 160.

27 Quoted in Mark de Lannoy, *The Kulasekhara Perumals of Travancore: History and State Formation in Travancore from 1671 to 1758* (Leiden: Research School CNVS, 1997), p. 28.

28 See de Lannoy, pp. 55, 123, 126.

29 Ibid. p. 130.

30 See ibid. p. 136, for example, where we read how the maharajah obtained the crown jewels of the Quilon and Tekkumkur rajahs by paying the Dutch, with whom these were pawned by those rulers in return for cash to help fight against Travancore.

31 Shungoonny Menon, p. 171.

32 Ibid. p. 289.

33 Incidentally, the model for these reconstructions seems to be the Adikesava temple in Thiruvattar, which has older versions of many of the same features, including an ottakal mandapam. So, if Padmanabhaswami is made of 12,008 saligrama, the Thiruvattar deity is made of 16,008; if the god in Thiruvananthapuram is 18 feet long, Adikesava can claim 22. The Thiruvattar structures are said to have been constructed by medieval Chola kings, so by imitating them in Thiruvananthapuram, Martanda Varma was signalling a matching claim to greatness. Of course, in terms of royal patronage, Thiruvattar, which was also within Travancore, paled in comparison to Thiruvananthapuram.

34 The scholar Caleb Simmons has studied this phenomenon in detail for the Mysore kingdom in his *Devotional Sovereignty: Kingship and Religion in India* (New Delhi: Oxford University Press, 2020).

35 Reference is to Maharajah Swathi Tirunal Rama Varma (r. 1829–46), who was also a poet.

36 Shungoonny Menon, pp. 174–75. Ever the realist, another command the dying maharajah issued was to never break the alliance with the British!

37 See Civil Appeal No. 2732, Sri Marthanda Varma vs State of Kerala, judgement dated 13/07/2020, Supreme Court of India (Diary Number 10179-2011).

The Brihadisvara Temple in Thanjavur: The Lives of a Chola Masterpiece

Indira Viswanathan Peterson

No matter from which direction one approaches Thanjavur, one's gaze is irresistibly drawn to a colossal, elegantly ornamented temple tower presiding over this renowned city in south India's Kaveri delta region. A closer look at the soaring structure confirms its identity as the central 'vimana' rising above the sanctuary (garbhagriha) of a palpably ancient shrine. Built by Rajaraja I (reigned 985–1014) in 1010 CE at his kingdom's capital, the Brihadisvara temple is a masterpiece of Chola architecture and an icon of Tamil religion, art, history and culture. The grandest granite structural temple in the Dravida style as developed by Rajaraja and his successors, this magnificent abode of Shiva was placed on UNESCO's list of world heritage sites in 1987, and is one of south India's premier tourist attractions. For Shiva's Tamil devotees, however, the shrine is simply the Big Temple, ('periya koyil'), a beloved, vibrant place of worship. Rajaraja's temple is that rare thing, an ancient monument and architectural marvel, that is at the same time a living temple.

The publication, at the beginning of the twentieth century, of the Tamil inscriptions that cover the walls of the Thanjavur temple catapulted it into fame as a key resource for recovering the history of the illustrious Cholas, who nurtured a great flowering of Tamil civilisation. Nevertheless, thriving under the patronage of the Pandya, Nayaka and Maratha kings, who ruled Thanjavur after the Cholas, the monument abundantly reflects the legacies of later golden ages as well.[1] The Brihadisvara temple is in fact a palimpsest of the multicultural histories of more than a thousand years of worship and artistic endeavour, conveyed to us across time through inscriptions, ritual traditions, sacred hymns and stories, and processions of images of gods and saints, as well as through painting, sculpture, poetry, music, dance and drama in many languages. To visit this temple is to plunge into the world of Thanjavur and the Kaveri delta as a perennial centre of Shaiva religion and Tamil regional culture.

Rajaraja's temple: A journey in time

Entering the temple campus through its three eastern gateways (an unpretentious later gateway rises from the fortified walls that enclose the monument, followed by two imposing ones dating to Rajaraja's time), the visitor walks into an immense rectangular courtyard edged by a colonnade, dominated by the sanctuary tower, and sparsely populated by smaller shrines, and immediately takes a step back in time. Other major south Indian temples—Chidambaram and Madurai, for example—have grown into mega complexes over the centuries, crowded with increasing numbers of enclosing walls, shrines and ornate mandapam halls, and ever-taller gopuram gateways. The Thanjavur temple, by contrast, remains a serene, vast sacred space, reflecting to this day the uniqueness of its royal founder's vision of the glorification of Shiva.

The Big Temple is a monument of superlatives in every respect. Grandeur of size and scale, mathematical and geometric precision, and innovative symmetries of proportion that draw on and yet transcend the prescriptions of the early Shaiva Agama texts give Rajaraja's temple its distinctive ambience. The dimensions of the walled courtyard, the main temple and the central deity are merely three examples of these features. The compound is a perfect double square, measuring 241 x 121 metres, and its proportions are echoed in several of the temple's architectural elements. The linga sanctuary measures 24 metres square externally. Based on a high platform, the vimana tower rises to a height of 59.82 metres from the ground, dwarfing the tallest of the gopura gateways. The tower's 13 square storeys of diminishing size form a pyramid that culminates in an octagonal domed shikhara pinnacle. The pinnacle sits on a 26 metre square granite slab weighing 80 tons, and is capped with a massive gilded copper pot finial. In Rajaraja's days, the Thanjavur vimana was the tallest temple tower in India. Likewise, measuring 1.9 metres in diameter and 3.95 metres in height (including the pedestal), the image Rajaraja installed in the sanctuary is among the largest Shiva lingas worshiped in a temple. The king called the deity 'Rajarajesvaram Udaiyar', (the Lord of Rajaraja's temple) in Tamil, but the name was later replaced by 'Brihadisvara', the Sanskrit version of the Tamil 'peruvudaiyar', the great Lord. His consort is Brihannayaki.

The stories of gods, devotees and saints sculpted in stone and stucco on the great gateways look as vivid as they might have appeared on the day the temple was completed, and the central shrine platform's walls and stairways are covered with small sculptures as well. These are beautiful, but the large-size sculptures of Shiva's murtis—his manifest forms—that are carved in the vimana's outer wall niches at two levels are masterpieces of Chola art. They come into view as we circumambulate the temple. My personal favourites are Nataraja (the cosmic dancer), Kalantaka (vanquisher of the god of death), and Bhikshatana (Shiva as the mendicant beggar) on the south wall, and Ardhanarisvara (Shiva conjoined with his consort) on the north wall. The tower also houses a hidden treasure, a series of large paintings on the walls of the passageway enclosing the inner sanctuary. These exquisite frescoes came to light only in 1931. Depicting various manifestations of Shiva, scenes from the life of the poet-saint Sundaramurtti Nayanar, and Rajaraja and his queens worshipping the Lord, they are rare specimens of Chola painting. Conservators have managed to remove and preserve the Nayaka-period works that were painted over the Chola frescoes.

In Rajaraja's time, the other deities prescribed for worship in Shiva temples were housed in shrines and niches along the Brihadisvara's enclosing colonnade. Among the separate shrines in the courtyard, only that of Shiva's steward, the saint Chandesa, dates from the founding of the temple. In subsequent centuries, Pandya and Nayaka rulers added shrines and mandapa pavilions for Nataraja and the goddess, and a Nayaka king built a beautiful temple for Subrahmanya, counted among the finest examples of Nayaka architecture. Without detracting from the main temple's majestic beauty, this highly ornamented structure offers intimate encounters with the narratives of the gods, especially of Skanda-Murugan, in its finely chiseled sculptures.[2] The latest additions are a plain Ganesha temple built by the Maratha king Serfoji II, and a small twentieth century shrine for Karuvur Devar, the Chola era poet-saint who extolled Shiva and the Thanjavur temple in a Tamil hymn in *Tiruvisaippa* (Sacred Songs): 'How marvellous, how beautiful the form, bright as a hundred million rising suns, worshipped by the whole world, the form of the Lord who dwells in Rajaraja's temple in Thanjavur, enclosed by walls outfitted with leaf-covered ramparts, and abounding in fortified towers of many tiers, lofty as mountains, touching the white moon!'[3] Lastly, the massive monolithic image of Shiva's bull, Nandi, installed by a Nayaka patron in the pavilion facing the sanctuary, takes pride of place among the later additions to the temple. Along with Rajaraja's vimana, it has become an icon of the Brihadisvara temple.

Chola history and Shaiva devotion at the Brihadisvara temple

Legends about the Cholas and the Brihadisvara temple, the most spectacular and enigmatic of the Kaveri delta temples, circulated in popular oral and written traditions long after the Chola era. The *Brihadisvaramahatmya* (The Glorification of the Brihadisvara Temple), a late Sanskrit purana text, tells us that the temple's founder was a certain Karikala Chola, and describes the miracles that enabled the monument's construction and its ceremonial consecration. Karikala brought a naturally formed banalinga from the Narmada river and installed the deity in the sanctuary of the Thanjavur temple, built at his command by a father and son team of master architects from Kanchipuram. The construction was suspended when a stone large enough to support the shikhara at the top of the vimana could not be found, but was resumed when a huge monolithic slab was provided by a poor old woman at Shiva's behest (we know now that the slab is a composite). The great stone bull is the subject of the most popular legend about the temple, also narrated in the *Mahatmya*. The Nandi kept growing bigger, until the architect nailed it down after tapping its thigh and expelling a toad that had been living inside. Clearly, our predecessors were as intrigued as we are by the feats of size and engineering skill involved in the construction of this temple, including the mystery of how the granite required for the building was transported, when the nearest source of the stone is several kilometres from Thanjavur, a city situated in a flat riverine plain.

While some of the temple's enigmas may never be solved, the more than 107 Tamil inscriptions on the temple walls, the majority of which were commissioned by Rajaraja and his immediate successors, are a treasure trove of historical information. A fascinating window into Rajaraja's illustrious career, his devotion to Shiva, and Agamic temple worship in medieval Tamil Nadu, the inscriptions also record and describe in minute detail the economy and administration of the Thanjavur temple as envisioned by the king. Such systematic, comprehensive documentation from the founder's days is not available for any other south Indian temple. The information provided here ranges from the exact weights of precious gems, to the specifications of the images made for worship in the temple's many sub-shrines, to the names, tasks and earnings of every one of the men and women who served as functionaries at the temple. We learn above all that the Thanjavur temple was a royal monument, meticulously planned by Rajaraja, and bearing his stamp in every detail. In addition to celebrating all the festivals of a Shiva temple, the linga at Rajarajesvaram was honoured with a ritual bath (abhiseka) on the day of Rajaraja's natal star (sadayam) each month, and more elaborately in Aippasi, the month of his birth. The king's family and his religious preceptor, as well as his military officers and courtiers, were integral participants in the royal project. Rajaraja's grandson Rajendra III enhanced the temple's grandeur, and celebrated his grandfather in numerous ways, including the performance of *Rajarajanatakam*, a play in his honour.

The magnificence of the Thanjavur temple—it was styled 'Mahameru', a replica of the celestial mountain Meru—was an expression of its founder's imperial glory as well as his devotion to Shiva. Rajaraja had conquered all of South India, extended Chola authority over parts of Sri Lanka, and taken over the Maldive islands.[4] He assumed the title Rajarajadeva, 'king of kings', but also called himself 'Shivapadasekhara' (he who bears Shiva's feet as his crown), and gifted the gold and jewels captured in his conquests toward the construction and maintenance of the Thanjavur temple and the worship of Shiva and the other deities he installed there.[5] It comes as no surprise that the emperor and his entourage showered the temple with the most lavish gifts and endowments, or that every one of these was recorded in stone. Here is Rajaraja's command: 'Let the gifts made by us, those made by our elder sister (akkan), those made by our wives, and those made by other donors ... be engraved on stone on the sacred shrine (srivimana).'[6] Among the dazzling gifts were sixty-six metal images of deities, outfitted with jewellery crafted of gold and priceless gems.[7]

Along with artistic elements at the temple, Rajaraja's inscriptions offer tantalising clues to his personal vision of

Shiva. Adavallan (Expert Dancer), a second name given to the Lord at Thanjavur, suggests that the king conceived of Brihadisvara as identical with Shiva as the Cosmic Dancer at the temple in Chidambaram, the tutelary shrine of the Cholas. The space above the Thanjavur sanctuary connects with the concept of cosmic space, 'paramakasa', the supreme mystery of Shiva's dance in Chidambaram. In addition to large mural paintings of the dancing Shiva, the Lord himself is depicted as dancing, employing 81 of the 108 Karana dance postures described in Bharata's *Natya Sastra,* in a series of reliefs sculpted on the upper level of the passageway around the sanctuary. So great was Rajaraja's devotion to the dancing Lord that the principal measure employed for weighing gifts and other materials at his temple was also named Adavallan.[8]

Shaiva devotion and temple worship in the Kaveri delta were stimulated and immeasurably enriched by the moving Tamil devotional (bhakti) hymns of the three great Nayanar poet saints, Appar, Sambandar and Sundarar, who flourished in the Pallava era (sixth to eighth centuries). Rajaraja's temple became the site of the grandest celebration of the saints and their hymns, collected in the *Tevaram* anthology. The Nayanars were revered in bronze images, and forty-eight 'pidarar' singers were appointed for performing their hymns, accompanied by drummers. Surpassing all other patrons, Rajaraja also recruited from various temples, four hundred 'women of the temple quarter', ('talichcheri pendir'), in this case dancers, to serve at the Brihadisvara temple. The relevant inscription records not only the names and places of origin of each of these women, but also the streets where they were housed, and the land, grain and other emoluments allotted to them.[9]

The statistics of the material and human resources allotted

for ritual and maintenance at the temple are staggering. For example, 2,832 cows, 1,644 ewes and 30 buffaloes were distributed to 366 cowherds, who were required to supply ghee (for burning lamps) at the temple. The details given in many inscriptions feast the senses and the imagination. We can almost smell the water, scented with champaka buds, khas-khas roots, cardamom seeds and other substances used for bathing the linga, and we marvel at the subtle distinctions made among the pearls used in the jewellery the king's revered sister, Lady Kundavai, offered to the goddess; there were round pearls, roundish pearls, polished pearls, pearls of red water, unpeeled pearls, and many more kinds, harvested from the peninsula's pearl fisheries. But the greatest thrill the inscriptions offer is the opportunity to 'meet' the more than 850 functionaries, from the chief architect to the lowliest watchman, who made Rajaraja's temple the wonder that it is.

European romance, and a Maratha renaissance

Throughout its history, Lord Brihadisvara's temple was a cherished place of worship for Thanjavur's rulers. In the eighteenth century, however, the Maratha Bhonsle kings became increasingly embroiled in the politics of the Carnatic, which was dominated by the rulers of Mysore and Arcot, and by competing European trading companies. By the reign of Tulajaji II (reigned 1763–73 and 1776–87), Thanjavur, politically subordinated by the English East India Company, had become colonial 'Tanjore'. The inevitable happened. From 1777–98, during the Mysore wars, a British garrison occupied the Brihadisvara temple's precincts, and worship was reduced to a bare minimum. There was no question of the kind of upkeep demanded by a great Hindu temple.

However, the air of decay that pervaded the temple at the time proved strangely alluring to British visitors. Where devotees saw a living temple being desecrated, engineer-surveyors Elisha Trapaud and Michael Topping, as well as touring artists such as Henry Salt, viewed the 'Great Pagoda' of Tanjore through a romantic and antiquarian lens, as a picturesque ruin. Their paintings and drawings of the temple circulated widely among European audiences, but the most celebrated of these depictions is undoubtedly that of the artist duo Thomas and William Daniell, who toured India in the late eighteenth century, immortalising its great monuments and landscapes in their enchanting aquatints.[10] The Daniell painting of the 'Great Pagoda' remains a conversation piece with connoisseurs worldwide.[11]

But the Big Temple was not condemned to remain a sleeping princess forever. It was rescued at the turn of the nineteenth century by Serfoji II (reigned 1798–1832), Tulajaji's adopted son. Within a year of attaining the throne, the English-educated Serfoji was pensioned off by his British overlords, his sovereign rule restricted to a severely truncated 'Tanjore kingdom', consisting of just the fort-city of Thanjavur and the Brihadisvara temple, located in the 'Small Fort'.

My own romance with the Big Temple blossomed from my fascination with Serfoji's genius and his remarkable contributions to south Indian culture, achieved under the most abject circumstances. A polymath and innovator, the Maratha king forged a glorious cultural renaissance at Thanjavur, one that reflected the city's ambience as the confluence of multiple linguistic and ethnic streams and fundamentally reshaped arts and learning in modern South India.[12] The Brihadisvara temple was a focal point for Serfoji's renaissance. What intrigued me the most were the uncanny resonances of Serfoji's actions at the temple with those of Rajaraja, even though the Chola king's inscriptions had not yet been deciphered.

For Serfoji, as for Rajaraja, the Brihadisvara temple was the king's own temple. While he could not match the Chola emperor's munificence, Serfoji restored the temple to its former splendour, and added greatly to its cultural riches. Making a pilgrimage to the major Kaveri delta temples, he styled himself monarch of the Chola land (Cholabhupati). He collected 108 lingas from distant shrines, and established them in the Brihadisvara temple colonnade. He recorded his contributions in Marathi inscriptions at the temple, as well as in a Marathi poem, *Sarabhendratirthavali*. He also inscribed on the colonnade walls a long Marathi text, the *Bhomsalavamsacaritra*, a history of the Thanjavur Marathas. With these acts, Serfoji both expressed his devotion to Brihadisvara and recentered his sovereignty in Thanjavur, in symbolic defiance of colonial domination.[13]

An avid patron of new painting styles, Serfoji commissioned paintings for the ceiling and walls of the goddess shrine; the legends of Madurai were painted on the colonnade walls.[14] In addition to promoting the Sanskrit *Brihadisvaramahatmya*, along with a Tamil translation, Serfoji commissioned a Chola-style *Ula* poem in Tamil, describing Brihadisvara's festival procession.[15] Serfoji's greatest contribution, though, was his vigorous promotion of the performing arts at the temple. The king made the temple's mandapas and courtyard ring with the festive sounds of drama, dance and music, in Telugu, Tamil, Marathi and Sanskrit. Under his patronage, the Tanjore Quartet, brothers who were gifted composers and dance masters, composed numerous padams, varnams, svarajatis, tillanas and other musical and dance pieces on Brihadisvara, the goddess, and the king. These were performed by singers and devadasi dancers at the temple as well as the royal court. The Quartet's compositions spread Thanjavur performance traditions in other south Indian courts, and became an important part of the Carnatic music and Bharatanatyam dance repertoires that were eventually refashioned in Madras city (now Chennai). But the *tour de force* among the works commissioned by Serfoji for the Big Temple was *Sarabhendrabhupala Kuravanji*, an innovative Tamil dance drama which portrayed the glory of both Serfoji and Lord Brihadisvara through the songs and dances of a Kuravanji (aka Kuratti), a wandering tribal fortune-teller.[16] This highly popular drama was performed by devadasi dancers at the temple's annual festival, on a permanent platform ('Kuravanji medai'), erected by Serfoji in front of the Nandi pavilion.

Serfoji's son Shivaji II immortalised the Thanjavur Maratha dynasty in a portrait gallery in the vestibule of the Subrahmanya temple's pavilion. Sadly, the British government declared the Tanjore kingdom extinct in 1855, when Shivaji died without a male heir. Three years later, Linnaeus Tripe, who toured south India as government photographer, recorded striking views of the Big Temple in the new visual medium of photography. For Tripe, as well as for Edmund Lyon, Samuel Bourne and other British photographers who followed him, the Thanjavur temple was the relic of a vanished past, the symbol of a kingdom in ruins.

A new era for the Brihadisvara temple

A celebrated panorama photograph by Tripe, of the Chola inscriptions on the Big Temple's vimana, underscores their enigmatic quality. Ironically, not long after it was made, Tripe's image was folded into the project of cracking the Chola Tamil script. Epigraphists E. Hultzch and V. Venkayya succeeded in deciphering the script, and the text and translation of the Brihadisvara inscriptions were published at the beginning of the twentieth century. These, along with other texts and artifacts, stimulated the study of Chola history and art. By the 1930s the Big Temple became the premier space for experiencing the Tamil past. A Rajaraja Chola Museum was established at the temple, Rajaraja's birthday was celebrated as Founder's Day, and a statue of the king was set up in the temple precincts. The acme of these activities was the publication, in 1935, of historian K.A. Nilakanta Sastri's *The Cholas*. But it was the great modern Tamil writer Kalki's epic historical novel *Ponniyin Selvan* (The Son of the Kaveri), serially published in the 1950s, that brought the romance of Rajaraja and Cholas home to the Tamil public, just as Walter Scott's novels had conjured up the milieu of the Scottish Highlanders for his audiences.

The Brihadisvara temple's millennial anniversary was celebrated with éclat in 2010. Numerous books about the temple were published that year, and the Government of India issued a commemorative stamp, coin and currency note. Aptly, along with other events, the monument's founding day was celebrated with a performance at the temple by one thousand dancers. The Big Temple continues to flourish in the new era. The great Nandi continues to receive abhisekas, and the old 'ter', the festival cart carrying the deities in procession, has been refurbished and put to use. Devotees continue to flock to worship at the temple, mingling, as always, with the scholars, history buffs, artists, dancers, engineers, archeologists and others who stream in to partake of this ancient monument's eternal beauty and mystery, and to listen to the fascinating stories it tells.

Further Reading

Vidya Dehejia, *The Thief Who Stole My Heart: The Material Life of Sacred Bronzes from Chola India, 855-1280.* Princeton: Princeton University Press, 2021. The A.W. Mellon Lectures, NGA, Washington, D.C. Bollingen Series XXXV: Volume 65.

E. Hultzsch, *South Indian Inscriptions*, Vol. II, Parts 1-3, Madras: Government Press,1891-95.

George Michell, and Indira Viswanathan Peterson, *The Great Temple at Thanjavur: One Thousand Years. 1010-2010.* Mumbai: Marg, 2017 (second edition).

R. Nagaswamy, *Brihadisvara Temple: Form and Meaning.* Delhi: Aryan Books, 2010.

Indira Viswanathan Peterson, *Poems to Śiva: The Hymns of the Tamil Saints.* Princeton: Princeton University Press, 1989.

J.M. Somasundaram Pillai, *The Great Temple at Tanjore*, Madras: Solden & Co., 1935, reprinted Tanjore: Tanjore Palace Devasthanam, 1958.

B. Venkataraman, *Rajarajesvaram: The Pinnacle of Chola Art.* Madras: Mudgala Trust, 1985.

Notes

1 The Cholas of the Vijayalaya line ruled the Thanjavur kingdom from 850 to 1279 CE, the Telugu-speaking Nayakas, an offshoot of the Vijayanagara empire, from 1533 to 1674, and the Maratha Bhonsles, relatives of Chattrapati Shivaji, from 1674 to 1855.

2 The Nandi mandapa is graced by Nayaka period sculptures, as well as by Maratha era paintings.
3 Karuvur Devar, *Tiruvisaippa* 9.1 (Translation by Indira Peterson). The temple was connected to the king's palace, and enclosed by walls, in the Chola era. In the sixteenth century, Sevvappa Nayaka built a moated fort around Thanjavur city, and a smaller fort around the Brihadisvara temple.
4 One inscription reveals that the 'iluppai' oil used for ritual at the temple was brought from Sri Lanka.
5 Tripurantaka (Victor of the Three Forts), a martial form of Shiva, is portrayed in many places in the Thanjavur temple.
6 *South Indian Inscriptions (SII)*. Vol. 2. 1.
7 The majority of the Chola era images are lost. Only one icon, a dancing Shiva, remains in worship at the temple.
8 Dakshinameruvitankar, the name of the volumetric measure used at the temple, refers to Shiva at Chidambaram. Dakshinameru (Southern Meru), a name of the Chidambaram temple, is also applied to the Thanjavur vimana.
9 *SII*. Vol. 2. 66.
10 Edward Lear and Marianne North were two among many European artists who painted views of the Brihadisvara temple.
11 Be sure to look for the hatted European figure sculpted on the temple vimana—was he a European trader?
12 My book in progress on Serfoji is provisionally titled *Tanjore Renaissance: King Serfoji II and South Indian Modernity*.
13 The defiance could not be definitive: the temple fort's outer spaces were used for defence during the Napoleonic Wars, and in 1808 William Lambton used the vimana as a surveyor's platform.
14 Serfoji also commissioned European-style drawings of the temple and the bull.
15 Sivakkolundu Desikar's *Thanjai Peruvudaiyar Ula*.
16 This drama was also authored by Sivakkolundu Desikar.

Rhapsodies in Stone: The Temples at Belur and Halebidu

Meera Iyer

A long, long time ago, an ambitious king won a major battle against an arch-enemy. He commemorated this victory by building a beautiful temple, dedicated to Vishnu. Master sculptors, masons and architects were brought in to work on this royal monument, and they laboured ceaselessly and passionately on the project. The result was a grand and stunning new creation, built in a style never before seen. Just four years later, a second temple, dedicated to Shiva, was unveiled that further refined this new style.[1]

Nine hundred years later, these two temples, the Chennakeshava Temple in Belur, consecrated in 1117 CE, and the Hoysalesvara Temple, consecrated in 1121 CE, are still justly renowned for being among India's most exquisite works of art and architecture.

The Hoysalas: A new millennium, a new kingdom

The genesis of the Hoysala style lies in the establishment of a new kingdom, dynasty and state. At the dawn of the second millennium, the Kalyani Chalukyas reigned supreme over much of Karnataka, while further down south, the Cholas ruled over much of Tamil Nadu. The first Hoysala of some renown was Vinayaditya who ruled from 1047–98 CE. He was succeeded first by his son and then his grandson, both of whom died after very short reigns.

And so it was that in about 1106 CE, Vinayaditya's second grandson, the celebrated Bittideva ascended the throne. Like his predecessors, Bittideva was a vassal of the Kalyani Chalukyas. But he had visions for a grand imperial future for himself and his descendants as sovereigns of an independent kingdom.

Two major events mark his reign, both of which had political consequences with reverberations till today.

The first was a meeting with a philosopher. It was sometime early in his reign that Bittideva met Ramanuja, the Srivaishnava philosopher-saint. Ramanuja is said to have been persecuted for his religious beliefs by the Cholas, and fled to the Mysore region. The story goes that Ramanuja cured Bittideva's daughter of some hitherto incurable disease. The king then converted from Jainism to Srivaishnavism and also changed his name to Vishnuvardhana.

The replacement of Vasantika, the original patron deity of the Hoysalas, by Vishnu, was at least partly a move towards the legitimisation of Vishnuvardhana as a ruler. Regardless of the impetus, this event certainly marked a vigorous introduction and subsequent patronage of Srivaishnavism in these regions.[2] Vaishnavism remained popular with the elites in several subsequent dynasties, including the Vijayanagara kings and the Wodeyars.

A second defining event in Vishnuvardhana's reign was his defeat of the Cholas at Talakadu, in 1116 CE. Inscriptions extol him as the one who 'brought all points of the compass under his command'. Of his victory against the Cholas, one epigraph says he was 'skilled with the bow in reducing the pride' of the Chola governor and that the river Kaveri was fairly choked with the bodies of his enemies. Another colourfully declares that the very south wind was stopped because of having 'to fill the nostrils of the skulls of the enemies slain in Vishnuvardhana's expeditions of victory on the banks of the Kaveri!'

The victory at Talakadu was only the first of several territorial advancements made by Vishnuvardhana, who ruled until 1142 CE. But his dream of an independent kingdom was realised only by his descendants since he himself was never able to shed the Kalyani Chalukya yoke. In the 1200s, Hoysala dominions stretched from the Tungabhadra river in the north all the way to Madurai in the south. The end of the empire came in 1346 CE when Ballala III died fighting in a battle against the newly established sultanate of Madurai.

The old order gave way to the new, and soon, the Vijayanagara dynasty replaced them on the stage of history in south India.

Birth of the tiger-slayer

Even as Vishnuvardhana aspired towards an independent Hoysala kingdom, he set about forging a new identity for the fledgling dynasty and its kingdom, something that would be distinct from that of contemporary kingdoms.

It was during Vishnuvardhana's reign that the origin myth of Sala, the tiger-slayer, first appeared in inscriptions. According to this legend, a sage, sometimes identified as a Jain ascetic named Sudatta, at other times remaining unnamed, was walking in the forest with his disciple Sala, on his way to worship the

Goddess Vasantika. Suddenly, a tiger emerged from the trees, ready to spring at them. The ascetic commanded Sala to strike at the tiger, saying, '*Poy*, Sala! (Strike, Sala!)', whereupon Sala struck the tiger with a stick and killed it. And thus, says the legend, was the dynasty bestowed with the name 'Poysala' or 'Hoysala'.[3]

The image of Sala slaying the tiger became the symbol of the Hoysala dynasty. It was emblazoned on its banners and conspicuously placed in many of its temples. One can see large sculptures of it prominently placed near the doorways in the Chennakeshava Temple.

Outstanding universal values

A new vocabulary of temple architecture was an important facet of a new Hoysala identity. When Vishnuvardhana chose to commemorate his landmark victory against the Cholas by building the Vijayanarayana Temple, now better known as the Chennakeshava Temple, he helped fashion just such a new architecture.

What exactly was this new Hoysala idiom? How was it different from temple architecture elsewhere in India? What were its so-called 'Outstanding Universal Values' that made it worthy of protection and preservation, but also made it distinct from other sacred architecture elsewhere? These were some of the questions my colleagues and I tried to answer when, in 2019–20, the government of Karnataka tasked the Bengaluru Chapter of the organisation Indian National Trust for Art and Cultural Heritage (INTACH)—with whom I am associated—with preparing a nomination dossier to have the 'Sacred Ensembles of the Hoysalas' inscribed on UNESCO's list of World Heritage Sites.

A team that included architects, art historians, historians and urban planners then grappled with this subject. There followed some exhilarating months of discovery, brainstorming, field trips, and stimulating meetings with archaeologists, dancers, archaeologists-cum-dancers, historians, art historians, architects, architectural historians and heritage experts from India and abroad. As per UNESCO's guidelines, we compared Hoysala temple architecture with those from other contemporary dynasties in India and abroad. We tried to understand what the influences on their architecture had been, and explored the political, religious and social milieu in which the temples had been built.

After almost two years of immersion in the world of the Hoysalas, the entire team built a special and lifelong bond with the Hoysala temples, besides also building up a lifetime of memories—a quick check of the temples' acoustics by singing in them; the thrill of discovering a meaning behind a hitherto unknown sculpture in a temple; the 'ergonomic testing' of the 'kakshasanas' or balcony seats in every temple, in other words, napping on them! We also came to the rather surprising conclusion that, for all the reams of writing available on the temples and their sculptures, there was actually very little rigorous research on the Hoysala temples.[4]

Exploring the Hoysala oeuvre

The temple at Belur was built with the deep involvement of Vishnuvardhana and his queen, the accomplished dancer, Shantala. In building this new statement of a temple, Vishnuvardhana and his master architects naturally drew on their knowledge of temple-building traditions elsewhere. Of course, one of the strongest influences on Hoysala architecture was that of their predecessors and then overlords, the Kalyani Chalukyas. We also know from inscriptions that architects and artisans from Kalyani Chalukya territories moved to the Hoysala lands to work on the new temples. It also had an aesthetic that was markedly different from the Hoysalas' early rivals in the deep south, the Cholas. The early Hoysala rulers were quite familiar with the temple typologies of Malwa in present-day Madhya Pradesh, having sacked their capital, Dhar: one inscription boasts how Vinayaditya 'took [Dhar] as if the preliminary sip before feasting on the world of his enemies'.[5] Epigraphs also attest to the many merchants from other parts of India, including Kerala and Gujarat, who operated in Hoysala cities and built temples here.

Thus fully acquainted with temple architecture in different parts of India, Hoysala architects then made informed decisions and eclectic selections of features from other temple typologies which they then modified and complemented with their own particular innovations to create something that was uniquely and emphatically their own.

The royal and the royalist temples

When the Chennakeshava Temple in Belur was unveiled, one can imagine the sensation it must have caused. Here was a royal temple, certainly a statement, the likes of which had never been seen. It had a true stellate plan, meaning its sixteen-pointed plan was derived by imagining a square rotated on its axis three times. It stood on a high 'jagati', or platform; temples in north and central India have been built on jagatis since at least the eighth century, but here was a jagati that echoed the temple's stellate profile, a fairly novel idea that served to further accentuate the temple's zigzagging walls.

It had a towering shikhara which was also of a kind that was new in these parts. This quasi-Bhumija shikhara is no longer extant—it was dismantled in the 1880s.[6] But Bhumija-style shikharas still abound in the temple, on the many subshrines along the stairways and around the jagati. And most arresting of all, the temple was a sculptural extravaganza, featuring large and ornate carvings of gods, goddesses and other divinities on each and every indentation of the wall.

And just four years later, along came the monumental Hoysalesvara Temple in Halebidu. This Shiva temple was built by a merchant with strong ties to the king. It has two shrines, named cleverly, if obsequiously, after the royal couple as Hoysalesvara and Shantalesvara. In magnificence and novelty, it vied with the Chennakeshava Temple. Together, these two temples, 16 kilometres apart, established the new Hoysala style that was then used in several hundred temples built over the next 150 years or so of the dynasty's rule. While the earlier temple set the basic framework for Hoysala temple architecture, several ideas from the Halebidu temple inspired additions in Belur.

Take for example the famed 'madanikas' of the Belur temple, supremely decorative bracket figures that purportedly support the eaves. There are forty-four of these figures surviving, four of them inside, the rest on the outer walls. Undoubtedly the jewel in the Chennakeshava Temple's crown, they were an afterthought, added sometime after the temple had been completed, perhaps by order of Vishnuvardhana himself. You can still see the original smaller brackets (carved with Hoysala tigers) behind some of the madanikas. The Hoysalesvara Temple also has a few madanikas surviving which were clearly part of the original scheme of decoration. Perhaps these were the inspiration for their more famous counterparts in Belur?

Creative genius

The exuberant horror vacui and the sheer ornateness of the Hoysala aesthetic can overwhelm visitors to the temple. It is difficult not to descend into purple prose when talking about the visual feast that is a Hoysala temple! I shall do so right away: it is no exaggeration to say that Hoysala sculptures are some of the most exquisite expressions in stone ever produced.

Analysing the temples with a cool head and an art historical gaze, several things can be considered unique, beginning with the stunning multi-course 'adhisthana' or plinth, a Hoysala invention that remains unparalleled.

Perhaps you could look at the antecedents of plinth courses to trace this Hoysala innovation. Dravida temple plinths usually comprise several courses including a 'padma' or inverted cyma recta moulding, a 'kumuda' or torus, and a 'kapota' or bird beak moulding. Similar mouldings though more decorative were also used in Nagara temples. In the early eleventh century, temples in Gujarat began featuring two decorative courses in their plinths, a lower course called a 'gajathara' featuring elephants, and a second course depicting humans, and hence called a 'narathara'. And then, like punctuated equilibrium in evolutionary biology, there appears the fully featured, multi-tier Hoysala adishthana—visually arresting yet also filled with meaning.

Numinous beauty

Just as stained glass in medieval churches conferred a numinous beauty on the structure but also served to tell stories from the Bible, so too the embellishments in Hoysala temples served to enhance a worshipper's experience at the temple.

There is symbolism imbued in the very conception of the Hoysala temple walls, and at multiple levels. Our team's art historian, Sarada Natarajan, pointed out how the adhisthana is a microcosm of the world and its living beings. On the lowest tier are the elephants which, figuratively, bear the weight of the temple on their backs as they march steadily on.

Up next is a band of stylised lions, each a metaphor for royalty and power. Then comes a course of horses with their riders, prancing, trotting, galloping, together representing speed and military superiority. Above and below the tier with horses are bands of sinuous floral creepers which serve to remind us of the abundance of the bountiful earth.

The next register, the cynosure of most eyes, is the narathara, the band featuring humans in the form of narratives depicting stories from the Ramayana, Mahabharata and the Bhagavata Purana.

Above these terrestrial beings is a course of makaras or stylised crocodiles, creatures of the waters that hence also symbolise life-giving rains.

Hamsas or swans—creatures of the air—occupy the topmost register. And above the biosphere encapsulated in this multi-tiered adishthana are the life-sized and larger sculptures of gods and goddesses, the heavenly realm.

Stories from the two epics have long been a favourite with sculptors working on temples. But in the Hoysala temple, these stories are made an important part of the 'pradakshina' or ritual circumambulation of the temple that all devotees undertake. The stories from the epics and the Bhagavata Purana are intentionally placed at a level which makes them easy to 'read'. Devotees can thus actively engage with the stories which unspool as they perform the pradakshina. Worshippers are similarly meant to engage with the sculptures of the gods and goddesses on the walls above the mutlilevel plinth as they circumambulate the temple.

This continuous series of sculptures of gods, goddesses, dancers, attendants, musicians and other divinities that clothes the outer walls is the Hoysala temples' piece de resistance, and another of the Hoysala architects' novel ideas. Each deity stands under a floral or vegetal canopy and is enshrined under pilasters and ornate models of temple towers.[7] Particularly in the Hoysalesvara Temple, the entire wall serves as the artists' canvas, as sculptures merge seamlessly one into the next, leaving no wall space unadorned or indeed visible in between.

There are hundreds of these large sculptures, nearly six hundred in the Hoysalesvara Temple alone. Each one of them could be considered a masterpiece. Some of my particular favourites are the Govardhanadhari, where Krishna lifts the Govardhan mountain to shelter people from the rain; the Venugopala image showing Krishna playing the flute; and the dramatic Ravananugrahamurti showing Ravana lifting and shaking Mount Kailasha.

These scenes are shown in both the Chennakeshava and Hoysalesvara temples but are rendered slightly differently in each. All three are busy panels, alive with people and animals. Little details emerge as you gaze at the images. You notice the snakes dangling from the base of the mountain in both the Govardhanadhari and the Ravananugraha panels, dislodged and lifted out from their underground abodes along with the mountain. You notice the deer listening to Venugopala's flute, their upturned heads gazing raptly at Krishna, even as some women nearby seem to sway to the music. You spot the trees and plants growing on Mount Kailasha, the guardians of the eight directions, different episodes in the story, all crammed into the space of the mountain. And you wonder whether the Hoysala propensity to carve scenes that so throb and thrum with life was a reflection of the teeming diversity of the Western Ghats' forests around them.

The pursuit of perfection

The madanikas of Belur have inspired much wonder, and even poetry: Kannada poet D.V. Gundappa's *Antahapura Geethegalu* is a set of poems about Belur's madanikas. Most of these sculptures in the round depict women (only three madanikas feature men) in the act of hunting, dancing, getting dressed or playing an instrument. Each sculpture perfectly captures a moment in time full of movement and controlled energy. Take, for example, a madanika on the south-eastern wall depicting a maiden being bothered by a monkey pulling at her garment. The damsel is shown turning around to shoo the monkey away. The sudden movement sends her garlands and long plait of hair swinging to one side, pulling slightly away from her body. Surely, the master artist (in this case, the sculptor Dasoja) was also a keen observer of human anatomy and movement to have rendered this motion in stone so perfectly.

Attention to detail and ornateness are of course hallmarks of Hoysala sculpture. Madanikas, gods, attendants, door guardians and others are all richly endowed with sumptuous headdresses and jewellery, and no detail, not a bead on a necklace nor a lock of hair nor the fold of skin on an upturned foot was too small to be overlooked by the Hoysala artist. In the adhisthana friezes, features such as suspensions on chariots, wheel spokes, warriors' weapons and flags have been delineated, enabling historians to draw inferences on transport vehicles and military technology in the Hoysala period. Artists also delighted in hyperreal details and diverting minutiae, such as lizards inching up a plant near an unsuspecting woman, miniature flies sitting on a tiny fruit, birds peeking out from behind some trees, and so on.

The Hoysala penchant for profusion of detail and elaborate embellishments was made possible partly by the choice of stone they worked with. Hoysala temples are built with chloritic schist, a kind of soapstone that is relatively soft when freshly quarried and gradually hardens with exposure.[8] Yet, even though many Kalyani Chalukya temples were built with the same material, it is the Hoysala artists who fully explored the potential of schist. They chiselled, carved and undercut the stone with consummate ease to produce sculptures in high relief, combining technical mastery over the material with a creative genius in translating stories and beliefs into stone.

A good illustration of such ingenuity is the depiction of the Chakravyuha episode from the Mahabharata, shown in the frieze on the adhisthana of the Hoysalesvara Temple. Here, the brave young hero Abhimanyu enters a circular maze-like military formation that he is then unable to exit, and is eventually killed. While the rest of the frieze has scenes depicted at eye level, the artist has cleverly switched perspective to a bird's eye view to show the maze itself.

Artists also excelled in capturing the nuances of movement

such as the tension in a human body that is poised to let fly an arrow, or the ripple of a drummer's muscle or the twist in a swaying dancer. Indeed, dance and music are unusually prominent in Hoysala temples. Rhythm animates many of the sculptures here: the madanikas are shown in dance-like poses. Several gods and goddesses on the external walls are also depicted dancing.[9] It is as if the whole temple worships the deity through dance and music.

Inside the temple, a slightly raised round platform in front of the garbagriha (sanctum) would have served as the place where temple dancers—and perhaps also the Queen Shantala—performed their worship of the deity. The performance space is marked out by four circular pillars decorated with a series of sharp ridges that are interspersed with flat bands, the whole being polished to perfection. Were these pillars lathe-turned or could such flawlessness have been wrought just by human hands? The jury is still out on this one. Many historians believe these were made on some form of a lathe, likely using animal power, while others are convinced these pillars were entirely handmade.

Artistic agency

Happily for us, we are on much firmer ground when it comes to the artists behind the rest of the temple's fabulous decorations. Many sculptures in the two temples bear inscriptions recording the names of the artists who made them. Prominent among the many sculptors who worked here are Dasoja, his son Cavana, Birana and Masada.

The tradition of artists signing their works is not entirely unknown in medieval India. What is unusual about the Hoysala temples is the number of signed images that we have and the style of some of these epigraphs, which are written in language quite reminiscent of royal eulogies. For instance, one sculptor gives himself the title, 'a thunderbolt to the mountain of rival sculptors'. Such artistic agency points to the artists' pride in their work and also suggests they had a high standing in society. This is in marked contrast to the usual conception of the medieval Indian artist being an anonymous creator.

A tradition that lives on

The last temple of any renown built in the style first established by the Hoysala ruler Vishnuvardhana was the Keshava temple in Somanathapura, about 35 km east of Mysuru, built in 1268 CE by a military official under the then Hoysala ruler Narasimha III. In the approximately 150 years between the first temple at Belur and this last at Somanathapura, hundreds of temples were built in this style. Many of them still survive in various states of preservation in villages and towns all over Karnataka, especially in the Hassan, Chikkamagaluru and Mysuru districts.

By the mid-1200s, the kingdom had grown so large, it was split into two divisions for better administrative control. But infighting, weak rulers and powerful enemies dented the once powerful kingdom. In less than a hundred years after the Keshava temple was built, the last Hoysala ruler was killed and the dynasty ceased to exist. And with that, so did the unique temple architecture of the Hoysalas.

Over the next few centuries, south India was dominated by the flamboyant Vijayanagara dynasty and its feudatories. Just as the Hoysalas established a new temple architecture to reinforce their identity, so too did the Vijayanagara kings, who looked to the Cholas and elsewhere for inspiration. As a result, very little of the Hoysala temple tradition continued beyond them. Except for one important exception. The Ramachandra temple in the heart of Hampi is famous for how the story of Rama unfolds along the path of the pradakshina, a tradition popularised by the Hoysalas. This Hoysala innovation is also seen in several sixteenth and seventeenth century temples around Karnataka, including in coastal Karnataka and around Bengaluru.

Today, most modern south Indian temples are built in styles that are reminiscent of Vijayanagara's grand structures. Yet, the Hoysala artists and their work still have a strong presence in the memory and imagination of the people of Karnataka. Even today, there are patrons who want to build new temples in the Hoysala style. Temple idols are still often made in this style. And even today, almost every traditional sculptor in Karnataka still holds the Hoysala artists' work as the gold standard, a pinnacle of skill they dream of achieving.

Notes

1 For a general history of the Hoysalas, see S. Settar, *The Hoysala Temples, Volumes I and II*. Bangalore: Kala Yatra Publications (1992); and J. Derret, *The Hoysalas: A Medieval Indian Royal Family*. Oxford University Press (1957).

2 Royal patronage meant that several Vishnu temples were built in the Hoysala regions, many of which are important pilgrim destinations till today. Also, Ramanuja's relatively revolutionary practice of allowing non-Brahmins to enter temples probably also had an effect on practices in some temples such as at Belur, which incorporated days and rituals especially for people from 'lower' castes.

3 Epigraphia Carnatica Vol. V, Hassan taluk, Inscription no. 61.

4 Settar's seminal two-volume work is an exception. Kelleson

Collyer studied the Hoysala artists: *The Hoysala Artists: Their Identity and Styles*. Bangalore: Directorate of Archaeology and Museums (1990).

5 Epigraphia Carnatica Vol. V, Belur taluk, no. 58.

6 The term Bhumija means rising from, born of, or derived from the earth. Belur's shikhara, though strongly reminiscent of a Bhumija shikhara, was not structurally a Bhumija shikhara.

7 Interestingly, in the Chennakeshava Temple, the deities are all enshrined under Bhumija towers. In the Hoysalesvara temple, the models of temple towers, moved here to the upper third layer of the wall, are variations of Dravida, Nagara and Bhumija shikharas.

8 Schist falls between 3-5 on the Mohs scale of hardness; granite is at 6-7.

9 Incidentally, while the gods and the madanikas are shown in poses derived from the Natyashastras, dancers in the friezes are shown in poses from the folk tradition.

Continuity Amidst Change: The Virupaksha Temple at Hampi

Basav Biradar

There is a general tendency to label the city of Vijayanagara—popularly known as Hampi today—as a place of ruins. The absence of significant modern architectural interventions, and little to no inhabitation in the city's urban core and the sacred centre, has helped preserve the medieval character of this famous city, thus adding to the 'abandoned' look and feel. Further, the stunning and rugged landscape, with its rocky hills, intriguingly shaped and coloured granite boulders, and the gracefully flowing river Tungabhadra seems to form the perfect backdrop for the monumental remains of a great medieval empire. No wonder then, that the first English language guidebook to Vijayanagara, written by the British archaeologist A.H. Longhurst in 1917 was titled *Hampi Ruins.* Some might even say it was the British *romance of the ruins* that convinced Colonel Colin Mckenzie and Co. to carry out extensive survey of the place in 1799. While this narrative of ruins is a convincing argument in the context of the Vijayanagara empire and its famous architectural remains, it does not take into consideration the mythical and religious associations that have contributed to a cultural continuity from much before the establishment of the empire, till the present day.

Researchers have discovered that the earliest reference to this region is in a seventh century CE inscription describing the donation by the Chalukyan king Vinayadithya, who was stationed in a camp at the Pampa tirtha, to a religious head. This finding indicates that the cult of river goddess Pampa existed here—Pampa being the mythical name of the river Tungabhadra—and was significant enough to be referenced by a king in an official document. The name Hampi, the hamlet where the Virupaksha temple complex is located today, is said to be derived from the local deity Pampa. Two other inscriptions from the tenth century CE, attributed to the Nolamba kings Udayadithyadeva and Irivanolambadhiraja, also mention the holy site of Pampa tirtha. One of these inscriptions also describes the king's donation to the deity of Mahakaladeva—otherwise known as Bhairava. Possibly, being a community goddess, the culture of devotion for Pampa involved practices—meat offerings, animal sacrifices etc.—similar to other such deities we see all over India. The presence of the cults of Pampa and Bhairava have led scholars to interpret the river crossing as a popular pilgrimage site for Hindu death rituals. Hence, it is likely that the earliest visitors to Hampi were pilgrims wanting to perform the last rites of their kith and kin. This interpretation also explains the name of 'Dakshin Kashi', meaning southern Kashi, that is often used to describe the stretch of the Tungabhadra here.

I first visited Hampi as part of a two-day school excursion in the early 1990s. We were a large group of twelve-year-old boys accompanied by two of our teachers. The only distinct memories from that trip are of the liveliness we felt while shopping for cheap souvenirs in the Hampi bazaar and the delight we experienced on seeing the playful elephant and the crowd in the Virupaksha temple. I think we were relieved to find some clamour after spending the day visiting the numerous empty monuments in insufferable heat. More than two decades and many visits later, I have learnt to better appreciate the complex narrative—formed by the confluence of gods, goddesses, kings, empires, the ubiquitous art and architecture—of the Virupaksha temple complex and the Hemakuta hill. Here, I have realised, it is difficult to understand the real and the historical without knowing the mythical.

The best way to experience the layout of this Shaivite centre and its picturesque setting is to climb to the summit of Hemakuta hill from the southern side. The majestic double-storied stone gateway at the summit—known to tourists as the sunset point—is the perfect vantage point to get a panoramic view of the lush green agricultural fields, the irrigation canals and the monuments in the urban core to the south, the Krishnapura temple precinct encompassing the Krishna temple with its bazaar and the Lakshmi Narasimha temple to the south east, and the Nandi mantapa at the end of the broad streets of Hampi bazaar and the Matanga hill to the eastern side. More importantly, to the north lie the many shrines on the sloping Hemakuta hill and the grand Virupaksha temple complex on the southern bank of the Tungabhadra at the foothills. With a little bit of imagination, one can also visualise a pathway from the gateway on the summit, down the slopes of the hill, through the few remaining single-storied gateways and the Virupaksha temple enclosure walls, all the way to the south bank of the Tungabhadra river. The current boundary walls of the temple complex and its west to east orientation almost seem like a confusing visual obstruction to this imagination. Also visible from the summit is the stark contrast between the freshly whitewashed walls and gopuras of the Virupaksha and the several unpainted, antique-looking shrines on the Hemakuta hill. These observations are clear physical manifestations of the change of guard in Hampi, with Virupaksha temple becoming the religious focal point during the Vijayanagara rule.

The journey down the gentle slope of the hill is marked with several carved reliefs—of the divine figures of Rama, Lakshmana and Sita, and the Nandi and the linga from the Shaivite cult—on the rocky outcrop and small temples showcasing the pre-Vijayanagara era architectural styles. Notable among these, at the bottom of the hill, are the two temples built in local granite, in the Kadamba style, with an entrance porch with overhanging eaves. Both these temples have a columned central mantapa and three empty shrines with pyramidal superstructures. An inscription in one of these temples reveals that the temple was built by Kampilaraya—a local chieftain who ruled in the region till 1327 CE and tried to establish his own kingdom after the fall of the Hoysalas and Yadavas—in memory of his parents and a close relative. These memorial temples and the many carved lingas on this hill are a testimony to the existence of a practice of building commemorative shrines in the memory of dead relatives. This practice seems to have been discontinued during the Vijayanagara era.

From the current topography, it is evident that Virupaksha takes the centre stage as the primary deity in Hampi. But it is also known that the river cult of Pampa was revered here much before Virupaksha. So, when did this change? As per

Dr Philip Wagoner, an architectural historian, the cult of Virupaksha—an avatar of God Shiva, literally meaning the one with the uneven eyes—and a small shrine for the deity, came about only in the twelfth century. Before that there existed only a small temple for Goddess Pampa—built in the ninth century—to the west of the present day Manmatha tank, and a shrine for Mahakaladeva on the Hemakuta hill. This shift from Pampa, the local goddess as the main deity, to Virupaksha is part of a larger phenomenon of Sanskritising religious and mythical associations across south India in the medieval times. In essence, through this process of Brahminisation, the once independent and untamed female goddess was now under the control and protection of a powerful male deity, as his consort.

The mythical story which explains this change in Pampakshetra—another name for Hampi—is found in the sthalapuranas (local histories blending history and mythology) and in the champu-kavya (a genre of literature) titled *Girija Kalyana*, written by Harihara, a local Kannada poet of the twelfth century. The story goes that Virupaksha was seated in deep meditation on the Hemakuta hill when Pampa saw him while she was bathing in the river, and desired to marry him. After her attempts to arouse the meditating god failed, Manmatha, the God of love, was summoned to assist in the mission. Manmatha fired arrows made of flowers scented with love at the ascetic god. A disturbed Virupaksha woke up in anger and reduced Manmatha to ashes with the power of his destructive third eye. The force of this act was so powerful that it formed a dent in the rocky outcrop and resulted in a pond which is now known as the Manmatha Kunda and is located just outside the Virupaksha temple enclosure to the north. But by this time, Manmatha's arrows of love had had their desired impact on Virupaksha and he consented to the marriage with Pampa. Thus, Virupaksha or Pampapati (husband of Pampa), became the dominant deity in Hampi, reducing the indigenous cult of Pampa—now adopted into mainstream as a form of Parvathi—to secondary status. From then on, the Phala-Puje (betrothal or engagement ceremony) and Kalyanotsava (the marriage ceremony) celebrations became the two major annual festivals of Hampi.

For me, thinking of this large-scale transformation in the religious power in Hampi has often resulted in several questions: Was there no local resistance to this change from an indigenous local deity to a venerated Hindu male deity? Did the new cult, rooted in the ancient Hindu texts and traditions, disenfranchise some of the local communities? What if the people resisting this Sanskritisation did not have the agency to leave a written record of their opposition? Or was the change accepted across the society with open arms? But one thing is certain; this change of guard from Pampa to Virupaksha seems to have elevated the status of this erstwhile river crossing from a local pilgrimage site to a well-known Shaivite pilgrimage centre across south India. Historical records suggest that royal patronage also increased substantially from the twelfth century onwards in Hampi.

In 1336 CE, when the opportunity to establish their own kingdom came knocking on the doors of the Sangama brothers—Hakka and Bukka—they decided to legitimise their newfound empire by making offerings to the Virupaksha temple in Hampi and adopting Virupaksha as their official deity. They also adopted the god's name 'Shri Virupaksha' as part of their official signature, a practice which continued till the end of Vijayanagara rule in the sixteenth century. As the kingdom expanded and their fortunes grew, the patronage of the Sangama brothers towards Virupaksha also increased. Bukka Raya I planned and built the new capital city of Vijayanagara to the south of the temple. This royal patronage for Virupaksha continued without interruption under the subsequent Saluva, Tuluva, and even the Aravidu kings who ruled from Penukonda and Chandragiri in the late sixteenth and early seventeenth centuries. From a small shrine in the twelfth century, the Virupaksha temple grew to a gigantic enclosure with multiple shrines by the middle of the sixteenth century.

The Vijayanagara temple architecture is an eclectic mix of Chalukya, Hoysala, Chola and Pandya architectural styles. Tall pyramidal entrance towers or Rayagopuras replete with richly carved stucco figures and grand open halls with elaborately sculpted pillars are the most prominent features of the Vijayanagara school. Since there has been continuous construction activity in Virupaksha temple complex from the twelfth century onwards, there exist examples of Chalukya, Rashtrakuta and Hoysala architectural styles along with the Vijayanagara era structures. The main shrine here is dedicated to the linga associated with Virupaksha, which was built in the ninth century, in the Rashtrakuta style. Of course, due to the modern additions and renovations, and limited access, the original style is hardly visible. The other important shrines are those of his consorts, Pampa and Bhuvaneshwari, wherein the lathe-turned pillars carved out of schist stone are examples of the late Chalukya style.

Today, the enclosure, entered through the monumental entrance gateway with an over fifty-metre-tall tower, consists of two rectangular courtyards separated by another Rayagopura, and is populated with multiple pillared halls and shrines. The scene outside, just in front of the entrance gateway, is a glimpse of what it must have been like in the sixteenth century. There are vendors on foot/bicycles selling toys, flutes, eatables such as churmuri, mirchi bhajjis, spiced up slices of cucumbers, bananas and guidebooks. Then there are the multilingual tour guides eagerly seeking customers, and the footwear stand boys calling on every visitor to deposit their footwear with them. Even amidst this din, the imposing gopura, with its double-storied granite base, and the beautifully sculpted figures on each of the diminishing stories of the brick and lime plaster tower, calls for the attention of all visitors.

The first important Vijayanagara imprint inside the large outer courtyard is the fading royal emblem—a collage of the Varaha or a wild boar, the sun, the crescent of the moon and a dagger—sculpted on the granite base of the colonnade running along the enclosure wall. There are multiple interpretations of the emblem; while some say it symbolises the empire's allegiance to the three gods—Vishnu (Varaha is an avatar of Vishnu), Rama (the sun) and Shiva (crescent of the moon)—the local guides have more colourful and poetic interpretations. My favourite among what I have heard from guides is this: 'The Vijayanagara empire and its power will last as long as the sun, the moon and the earth (represented by Varaha) exist.'

The other notable structure in the outer courtyard is the hundred-pillared Kalyana Mantapa (marriage hall) built by the king Krishnadevaraya. The divine marriage of Virupaksha and Pampa is conducted in this hall during the annual Kalyanotsava. This mantapa has a spacious interior with an open hall in the middle surrounded by pillars with cut-out colonettes. Krishnadevaraya, arguably the most powerful of all Vijayanagara rulers, also commissioned the intermediate

Rayagopura which leads to the inner courtyard and the magnificent Rangamantapa (dancing or entertainment hall) in front of the main shrine. An inscribed stone slab, mounted at the entrance of the Rangamantapa, mentions that these architectural marvels were commissioned on the occasion of Krishnadevaraya's coronation, in 1510 CE. These grand new additions to the Virupaksha temple complex became the architectural templates for the subsequent temple construction projects in the capital city, thus establishing the Vijayanagara style.

Although the Vijayanagara kings patronised Virupaksha as the official deity, the Tuluva dynasty rulers seem to have shifted allegiance towards the Vaishnava sect from the late fifteenth century onwards. Temples dedicated to Krishna, Tiruvengalanatha, Lakshmi Narasimha and Vitthala were built under their patronage. It is interesting that even when they were building large Vaishnava temples, they continued their patronage to Virupaksha temple as evidenced by architectural additions during Krishnadevaraya's coronation.

Upon entering the inner courtyard, apart from the architectural grandeur of the cloistered halls and pillars with cut-out colonettes, the queue of devotees to get blessings from the resident elephant Lakshmi is what catches the eye. To add to the variety, there are always monkeys—in the local version of the Ramayana, the monkey kingdom Kishkinda is located just across the river Tungabhadra—feasting on the food offerings made by devotees to various shrines in the complex.

A short flight of stairs flanked by two intricately carved yalis—a mythical animal with the head of a lion and the torso of a horse—lead to the pillared open hall of the Rangamantapa;

these two yalis are unique as they sport a snout of an elephant, the ears of a fox and the hood of a peacock. These features are not usually seen in carvings of yalis elsewhere. While these two yalis at the entrance stand independently with their fierce protruding eyes and raised paws, the yalis carved onto the sixteen other pillars inside the hall feature armed soldiers riding them. Carvings of the other mythical animal Makara (mouth of a crocodile, trunk of an elephant and feet of a lion), scenes from the Puranas and numerous divine figures can be found along with the colonettes on the pillars.

The most remarkable feature of the Rangamantapa are the painted murals on the ceiling. These are the only remaining examples of Vijayanagara-era paintings in the capital city. Art historians have opined that even these, in their current form, are nineteenth century restored versions of the originals. These murals are divided into symmetrical panels from the western end to the eastern end with a beautifully carved lotus medallion in the middle. As with almost everything in the Virupaksha temple, the murals also focus mainly on the Shiva-Parvati wedding. The Girija Kalyana panel showcases the wedding scenes of Shiva and Parvati (Girija Kalyana) with the pantheon of Hindu gods, goddesses, the Yakshas, Gandharvas and other celestial beings in attendance. There are also panels featuring the Sita swayamvara from the Ramayana, the Rama-Sita wedding and the fantastic scene from the Draupadi swayamvara from the Mahabharatha, of Arjuna aiming his arrow at the fish's eye by only looking at its reflection in the water.

Other than these scenes from divine weddings, there are panels featuring the ashtadikpalas or the gods of the cardinal directions, Manmatha Vijay, the story of Manmatha disturbing the meditating Shiva, and Tripuranataka, the story of Shiva conquering three celestial cities of the demon Tarkasura with the help of gods. The artistic imagination of the Tripuranataka is particularly interesting with Shiva standing on a chariot made of Prithvi (earth) as its body and Suryadeva (the sun god) and Chandradeva (the moon god) as its wheels; he is using a holy mountain as the bow with the serpent Vasuki (Lord Shiva's ornament) and Lord Vishnu as the arrow; Brahma the creator is the charioteer; the three cities are shown as freestanding circles. More than the artistry of the painter, the mythical stories with their vivid imagination contribute to the fantastical nature of these murals.

But for the many pilgrims who visit this temple complex, the most important visit is to the main shrine where Virupaksha is housed in the form of a linga. A brass face mask adorns the linga. Often, since there is no direct entry from Rangamantapa to the garbagriha, pilgrims in a hurry fail to notice the fine features of this hall. After paying reverence to Virupaksha, they seek blessings from his two consorts—Pampa and Bhuvaneshwari—who are housed in small shrines to the north.

Exiting through another gateway with a gopura to the north leads one to the group of temples opposite the pushkarni (holy water tank) known as the Manmatha kunda. The ninth-century Durga Devi temple, which was originally the Pampa shrine, and houses the twelfth-century inscription detailing donations to Virupaksha, Pampa and Mahakaladeva, is the most important of these group of temples. On the first evening of the three-day long betrothal festival, the idols of Pampa and Virupaksha are carried around the Manmatha tank after sunset in a rectangular wooden mantapa decorated with lights and flowers. This celebration, known as Teppotsava, is quite popular among the devotees.

At the bare minimum, at least two different trips are required to experience the magic of this tiny temple precinct of Hampi (not the entire city of Vijayanagara). It is best to plan the first trip during the non-festive season and utilise it to understand the history and mythology, and to experience the art and architecture in detail. But the second visit should be planned either during the betrothal festival (Phala-Puje) in the winter or during the Kalyanotsava in the spring. This is when the whole ecosystem of the myths, the physical architectural elements of the temple complex, age-old cultural traditions and the devotees come together to bring the place alive. This is also when one gets to witness the idols of Lord Virupaksha and Goddess Pampa, carried about in a grand chariot procession with thousands jostling with each other to get a glimpse, from the Virupaksha temple to the end of the Hampi bazaar. For a brief period, Hampi is transformed to its original grand self. Domingo Paes, a Portuguese traveller who visited during the rule of Krishnadevaraya in the early sixteenth century, wrote about the chariot festivals and the bazaars being a part of all the major temple complexes in the capital city. Of the bazaar street in front of the Virupaksha temple, he wrote:

> In this pagoda (Virupaksha temple), opposite to its principal gate, which is to the east, there is a very beautiful street of very beautiful houses with balconies and arcades, in which are sheltered the pilgrims that come to it, and there are also houses for the lodging of the upper classes; the king has a palace in the same street, in which he resides when he visits this pagoda.

In those times, during the festival time, merchants would be allowed to set up shops in the mantapas on this broad street; and it was normal during the peak of the empire to see precious jewels and diamonds being traded here along with snacks and sweets. Many foreigners visited these markets to participate in these trade fairs and some others visited to witness the grandiose nature of the celebrations in the capital city of this large empire. But the Battle of Talikota in 1565—in which the Deccan sultanates came together to defeat the Vijayanagara regent Ramaraya and his armies—put an end to the glorious rule of the empire in the region.

After their victory, the Sultanate armies reached the capital city and launched large-scale loot and destruction. This resulted in irreparable damage to the city which has remained abandoned since then. The Deccan historian Mirza Ibrahim Al-Zubairi described the aftermath in his famous work *Basatin al-Salatin,* 'The Muslim army remained at Vijayanagara for about six months. To a distance of twenty leagues round the city everything was burnt and reduced to ashes.' This narrative of 'annihilation of Vijayanagara' has been canonised and used by early twentieth-century historians to label the Vijayanagara empire as the 'Hindu bulwark' fighting against the multiple Muslim kingdoms of the Deccan. But if what Al-Zubairi wrote were true, we would not have a single monument standing intact today, let alone the grand Virupaksha temple complex. A more serious examination of the pillage by the Sultanate armies has revealed that not everything was destroyed. While Vaishnava cults such as the Vitthala temple, Lakshmi Narasimha idol and Tiruvengalanatha temple suffered serious damage, the Virupaksha temple, the Kadalekaalu Ganesha, Sasivekaalu Ganesha and the temples on Hemakuta seem to have escaped the wrath of looting soldiers. Surprisingly, these structures have also been spared by subsequent looting efforts and acts of vandalism—mostly in search of hidden treasure—which continued to affect the city of Vijayanagara in the seventeenth and eighteenth centuries.

The popularity of the Hampi Virupaksha temple also attracted patronage by the colonial rulers who, in the first half of the nineteenth century, carried out repair and construction activities here. Longhurst mentions in his guidebook that the Kanakagiri Gopura to the north, opening to the Manmatha group of temples, was renovated under the patronage of the collector F.W. Robertson. Probably this is when the paintings on the ceiling of the Rangamantapa were also restored and altered, and the fifty-feet tall main entrance gopura constructed. Even today, it is not uncommon to find politicians and other VIPs in attendance during the festival time. In essence, this temple precinct continues to be an influential religious centre in south India. The daily religious rituals and the annual festivals in the Virupaksha temple continue uninterrupted, making it the only Vijayanagara era temple alive in Hampi today. This is the only place amongst the entire world heritage sites where shops thrive, auto-rickshaws, private transport and even state transport buses are permitted to ply albeit restricted to a designated area. The power of myths, religious beliefs and traditions is such that all these facilities have been allowed for the pilgrims. While the empires and kings are long gone, the divine continue to rule Hampi.

The existence of vast architectural and archaeological heritage in this medieval city was recognised by UNESCO in 1986 when the 'group of monuments in Hampi' were awarded the world heritage tag. While this accreditation helped attract an increasing number of tourists in the subsequent decades, the overzealous heritage management efforts of the authorities have also led to issues of forced displacement. People had, gradually over the years, taken over the mantapas in the chariot street or the bazaar opposite the main entrance of Virupaksha temple complex, and set up their businesses and residences. Shops selling pooja essentials, a variety of eateries, including those selling Korean and Chinese food, toy shops and jewellery stores were all part of this modern version of the Vijayanagara bazaar. This is the same bustling bazaar which was the main attraction in Hampi for us young boys during our school trip in the 1990s.

But, in 2012, following a court ruling, all the modern structural additions in the Hampi bazaar, and the people living in them, were deemed encroachments, and were asked to leave. They were then rehabilitated in a small village just outside of the main perimeter of the protected heritage site. Now, a sound and light show attempts to recreate the atmosphere of the sixteenth century Hampi during the state-sponsored Hampi Utsav.

Today, about 1,500 people live in the hamlet adjacent to the Virupaksha temple. The tensions between the authorities and the local communities continue to plague Hampi as the much talked-about 'Hampi Master Plan', which intends to regulate and guide developmental activities in the whole 25 sq km area (identified as the original Vijayanagara city expanse), moves into implementation phase.

The temple complex has become the epicentre of Hampi today, attracting tourists, pilgrims and researchers alike and invariably features first on most itineraries. But as many visitors immediately realise, a two-hour visit to this marker of more than a thousand years of cultural continuity can only provide a fleeting glimpse of the many intertwining narratives here. Instead, the immense tangible and intangible heritage of Hampi needs to be absorbed slowly, bit by bit, one layer at a time.

The Temple of Rudra

Shrenik Rao

A thousand years ago, South India witnessed internecine warfare. Several dynasties—such as the Pallavas, Rashtrakutas, Cholas, Chalukyas and Kakatiyas—in their quest for power and territorial expansion, waged wars against each other and tried to establish their supremacy over the region.

The Chalukyas, under the leadership of King Taila II (reigned 973–997 CE), ousted the Rashtrakuta dynasty and established themselves as the sovereign rulers of south-west India.[1] With Kalyana as their capital, the Chalukyas governed their vast empire—blessed with salubrious weather, fertile soils and abundant natural resources—by appointing loyal chieftains as their feudatories.[2]

Beta was one such chieftain.[3] Loyal, fearless and enterprising, Beta laid the foundations of the Kakatiya dynasty that ruled much of the eastern Deccan region—present-day Telangana, Andhra Pradesh, parts of eastern Karnataka and southern Odisha—for nearly three centuries.

Born in a family of Karma or Kamma (a Buddhistic term) peasants, Beta rose up the ranks and became a feudatory prince within the Chalukya empire.[4] His successor, Prola—an astute warrior known by the sobriquet, 'ari-gaja-kesari', meaning 'lion to the elephant-like enemies'—climbed up the ladder and became a high-ranking general of the Chalukya king, Someswara (reigned 1042–68 CE).[5]

Circa 1052 CE, the Chola king Rajadhiraja ransacked the Chalukya capital, Kalyana.[6] In retaliation, Someswara attacked the Chola capital, Kanchi, with the assistance of Prola. The Chalukya army triumphed and Someswara granted a hillock called Anumakonda to Prola as a reward for his contribution. Prola's successors, Beta II and Prola II, assumed princely status under the Chalukyas. Eventually, Prola II declared himself as an independent king.

Circa 1158 CE, Rudra Deva, (sometimes referred to as Prataparudra I by some historians) the eldest son and successor of Prola II, occupied the throne with Anumakonda as the capital of the Kakatiya kingdom. Rudra, 'strictly adhered to the policy of territorial expansion planned by his father. After his succession to the throne, he devoted all his energy and resources to safeguarding his independent status and to extending his dominion wherever possible.'[7]

A fearless warrior, Rudra waged wars against his political rivals and subjugated powerful kings; his brutal and unforgiving conquests instilled fear among his rivals. Legend has it that his enemies died as a result of the, 'bewilderment born of the fear produced by the prowess of Rudradeva'.[8]

By 1162 CE, Rudra had vanquished his enemies and expanded his kingdom. He conquered the Godavari delta in Andhra Desa and extended his rule over the whole of Telangana. Through his conquests, he 'realised to a great extent the ambitions of his father'. And with 'his military exploits and consummate statesmanship, he transformed the Kakatiya kingdom into the Kakatiya empire. His glorious military campaigns are engraved at Anumakonda in easy flowing and luxurious Sanskrit verse'.[9]

But Rudra was not a brute or barbarian. Far from it. He was an able administrator and a learned scholar. The Draksharama inscription, dated 1186 CE, refers to him as 'Vidya Vibhushana', meaning 'he whose adornment is education'. He showed great interest in languages and 'contributed greatly towards the formation of Telugu identity and culture. A great patron of art, architecture and letters, he subsidised men of letters and encouraged them to pursue their calling'. The Pillalamarri inscription of Nami Reddi, dated 1195 CE, describes him as, 'the resort and refuge of learned men, who regarded him with much affection'.[10]

However, Rudra's unrestrained power and exceptional administrative ability did not translate into religious and institutional legitimacy. Though his family had ruled the region for five generations—protecting the people, punishing the offenders and preserving law and order—Rudra, the most powerful Kakatiya ruler, was not bestowed with the divine right of kings.

Why? For centuries, kingship in India was based on the varna system, a hierarchical framework propounded by an ancient Hindu legal text, *Manusmriti*. Cloaked in the language of jurisprudence, the text prescribes a rigid, discriminatory hierarchy in which the king is considered divine but only a Kshatriya who receives Vedic initiation is eligible to become a king. Moreover, Brahmins, considered to be above the Kshatriyas in the hierarchy prescribed by the varna system, are forbidden from accepting gifts from a king who is 'not of proper royal lineage'.[11]

Rudra was not a Kshatriya. The origins of the Kakatiya dynasty from the 'Karma (Kamma) toilers'—who according to the varna system were considered Shudras—meant that the

Kakatiya rulers were not accepted as kings.[12] Not considered to be of 'noble birth' or of 'royal lineage', the Kakatiya rulers were placed beyond 'the solar and lunar races of Kshatriyas just as the Nagas and other tribal people'.[13]

Simply put, Rudra, being a Shudra, did not find a place in the upper echelons of the complex caste hierarchy prescribed by Vedic literature.

There is one more twist in the tale. The Kakatiyas worshipped Sakti Kakati, a Jain goddess, as their family deity. Legend has it that the Goddess Kakati blessed the Kakatiya family with a son born out of a pumpkin creeper; through her divine grace, he acquired extraordinary martial skills, established his rule and proliferated the great Kakatiya dynasty.

The fact that the Kakatiyas trace their mythical origin through Goddess Kakati meant that they could not be accommodated into the Hindu fold. As followers of Jainism—though the Kakatiya rulers, fluid in their belief systems, straddled between the worlds of Jainism and Saivism—they could not find a place in the varna system.

However, in the Kakatiya system of governance, kingship was not determined by Vedic rites of passage. The Kakatiya society—'fluid', 'dynamic' and 'socially mobile'— 'offered many opportunities for individuals to enhance personal reputations through their own accomplishments'. As the historian Cynthia Talbot writes, 'Social identities [in the Kakatiya system of governance] were linked to individual achievement. There were many opportunities for both travel and social mobility due to the prevalence of military activity, long distance trade and herding.'[14]

Empowered by a dynamic social structure under the Kakatiyas, peasants, recruited into the military, formed a new warrior class. A good warrior—regardless of birth—could get the title 'Nayaka' (leader). And connections forged through joint military activities acted as 'fundamental ligaments of [the] Kakatiya body politic'. Several 'Kakatiya inscriptions articulate a warrior ethos, where shared military exploits and the distribution of honours bound together lords and their subordinates.'[15]

***

As Rudra's military conquests multiplied, he accumulated enormous power. But even as the locus of power shifted towards him, he realised the futility of power without legitimacy. He knew that the legitimacy of a ruler—and the institutionalisation of sovereignty—emanated not from coercive methods of control or savage conquests, but from other sophisticated forms.

A pragmatic statesman with a shrewd understanding of the dynamics of power, Rudra understood the importance of religious institutions in translating power into authority. He knew temples legitimised power and could offer religious sanction to his political conquests. So, Rudra decided to build a temple that could legitimise his sovereignty, immortalise his legacy, and stand as a symbol of his glorious reign—until eternity.

A few years after he ascended the throne, circa 1162 CE, Rudra started building the grand Thousand Pillar Temple near his capital, Anumakonda. Star-shaped, the temple has a shrine for three Hindu deities—Shiva, Vishnu and Surya (the sun god)—arranged around a central hall. Similar to most Chalukyan temples, the 'Trikutalaya', meaning the abode of three deities, stands upon a high base, about 10 feet high.[16]

Measuring 102 feet x 82 feet, it is built of granite blocks put together without mortar.[17] Built using sandbox technology, the Thousand Pillar Temple is an earthquake resistant structure, which withstood violent upheavals over hundreds of years.[18]

The temple, adorned with exquisite sculptures, symbolises the glory of the Kakatiya rule. It shows the master craftsmanship of its master sculptors. The statue of the Nandi (bull), at the entrance of the temple, is chiselled in monolithic dolerite. It is considered to be the vahana (vehicle) and guardian deity of Kailasha, the home of Shiva. 'The temple's sculpture, especially the depiction of human activities, shows fresh charm, elegance and almost a metallic finish. The perforated screen pattern on the ranks of the door jambs, female figures in various dancing poses, besides the Chauri-bearers and Dvarapalas standing cross-legged, pulsating with life and movement, are all the supreme workmanship accomplished by the sculptor of the age.'[19]

Its bracket figures, carved on the dolerite in a three-dimensional form, give it a 'metal like finish with its lustre intact even after 800 years of construction'. The sculptures are 'so precise that a needle can be passed through these minute details of these sculptures'.[20]

The roof of the dancing hall (natya mandapa) is sculpted with images of Gayatri, the goddess of learning. As a dossier prepared by the Archaeological Survey of India states, the 'roof beams are decorated with lotus design and figure sculptures depicting mythological scenes from the Puranas'. It further says that 'every inch of the four entablatures which support the Natya Mandapa experienced the touch of the Kakatiyan master sculptor's chisel'.[21] Such was their beauty that the former Prime Minister of India P.V. Narasimha Rao wrote, 'The ornamentation of the pillars of the Mandapa, architrave of the antharala and the ceiling of the Ranga Mandapa are rich, subtle and fine like exquisite filigree work on gold or silver indeed.'[22]

Directly above the inner sanctum, where the deity is placed, they built stepped and storied pyramidal structures called vimana, a symbol of royal glory. The vimana, 'adorned with layers of horizontal bands' and decorated with a shikhara, is the most elegant and distinctive feature of the temple. A record from an inscription in the Rudreswara Temple, dated to 1213 CE, states: 'On the top of the temple shines distinctly the golden cupola illuminating the space of the sky, always having the brilliance of a vast sun's orb, standing on the lofty peak of the eastern mountain.'[23]

Built over four decades, the Thousand Pillar Temple is an architectural marvel of the medieval Deccan. It is, as a symbolic monument, a metaphor for power and dominion—an allegory that embodies the glory of the Kakatiya rule. As P.V. Narasimha Rao writes, 'Historians and pundits of architecture have attempted what may be termed a technical exposition of this remarkable structure. But they have failed to conjure up even a faint picture of the temple and its wealth of artistry and breathtaking beauty. What the eye sees, nothing else can fully convey.'[24]

***

The temple was not merely a place of worship. As the UNESCO Nomination Dossier says, it 'exerted much benevolent influence on the social life of the village. It developed into a great religious as well as an educational institution.'[25]

The Dossier adds, 'Its construction and maintenance offered employment to number of architects and craftsmen who vied with one another in bold planning and skillful execution. The making of icons in stone and metal gave scope to the talents of the best sculptors ... the daily routine gave constant employment to a number of priests, choristers, musicians, dancing-girls, florists, cooks and many other classes of servants. The periodical festivals like Shivaratri, Ekadashi etc. were occasions marked by fairs, contests of learning, wrestling matches and every other form of popular entertainment. It also served as a town hall where people assembled to consider local affairs or to hear the exposition of sacred literature.'[26]

As the chief patron and donor of the temple, Rudra found a ritual basis for his rule; religious patronage was his strategy to build alliances, gain legitimacy and establish himself as the suzerain.

And a few years before he died, circa 1194 CE, 'Rudreswara' was consecrated as the presiding deity of the temple; honouring the king's name with the title 'lswara' meaning supreme lord and originator. Since then, the temple came to be known as Rudreswara Swamy temple. Colloquially, however, the temple is known as the 'Veyi-Sthambhala-Gudi', meaning the Thousand Pillar Temple.

Historical evidence points to the fact that Rudra 'delighted in building magnificent temples in his dominions'. The Ganapesvaram inscription states that Rudra 'built in the towns of the enemies, whom he destroyed, a number of celebrated temples called Rudresvarams, called of course after his own name'.[27]

Following Rudra's example, his ministers, officers, nobles and their families constructed Trikutalayas with Shiva as the deity, and dedicated them to their king. Soon, the naming of a deity after the king became a widespread practice. As

G. Yazdani states, these temples 'were generously endowed with donations of land, and permanent arrangements were made to carry on daily worship and the performance of agamic rites in them. Thus many splendid fanes built in the Chalukyan style rose all over the country and as a consequence Telingana became justly famous as a veritable land of temples.'[28]

In most instances, the dedication of a temple to their overlord was explicitly mentioned in the foundation inscriptions with the phrase, 'in the name of'. Archaeologists and historians found that more than half of the newly established temples—55 per cent or 59 out of 108 temples—in the Kakatiya period followed this practice.[29]

After Rudra's death, his successors—brother, Mahadeva, and his descendants, Ganapathi Deva, Rudrama Devi and Pratapa Rudra—carried forward the practice of constructing temple complexes and dedicating them to their ancestors or family members. Particularly, Ganapathi Deva (reigned 1199–1262), known as the 'Kakatiya kingdom's greatest builder', expanded the Kakatiyan architectural, political and religious footprint. He shifted the capital from Anumakonda to Orugallu, built a stone wall around the city and established royal temples.[30]

Patronised by enlightened rulers, Kakatiyan temple architecture acquired great fame. It was known for its secular ethos, intricate detailing and politico-religious symbolism.

The Kakatiyan architects designed royal temples following the principles of *Vastu Sastra*, an ancient Indian doctrine of architecture. Though broadly similar, the temples differed based on the number of deities/shrines within them; the majority of the temples had three shrines—the Trikutalaya style—similar to the Chalukyan architecture. However, the

Kakatiyan architects also designed temples that served as shrines for one (Ekakuta), two (Dwikuta), four (Chatuskuta) and five deities (Panchakuta).

In a few cases, subsidiary shrines were also constructed in relation to the main temple structure. Another unique feature of the Kakatiya architecture is the stone walls and 'Kirti-toranas'—meaning 'portals of glory', which symbolise victory.[31]

***

The glory of the Kakatiya empire reached its peak under the reign of Prataparudra II (reigned 1289–1323), an able statesman and a learned scholar with a passion for poetry and architecture. The grandeur and magnanimity of his court was unlike any other regional kingdom. The early sixteenth century Sanskrit text, *Prataparudra Caritamu*, describes his court:

> With all these people of various skills serving him, and surrounded by five thousand attendants who showered him with gold and riches and sprinkled him with scented water from golden bottles, Prataparudra sat in the great assembly and ruled the kingdom, considering the petitions of the local lords and entertaining the requests of ambassadors.[32]

But sadly, the power and glory of the Kakatiya empire came to an end under Prataparudra II. Destiny played a cruel game; the evil eye cast its sinister glare. And the power, glory and riches of the Kakatiya empire caught the attention of invaders from North India.

In 1309, twenty years into Prataparudra II's rule, Allauddin Khilji, the sultan of Delhi, sent his slave-general, Malik Kafur, to invade the Kakatiya state. Allauddin Khilji did not want to annex or annihilate the Kakatiya ruler. Instead, his strategy was to force Prataparudra into a subordinate monarch, paying obeisance and royalties to Delhi.[33]

In mid-January 1310, Malik Kafur arrived at the Kakatiya capital and showered arrows for an entire month. As the Kakatiya defences fell, Prataparudra, seeking peace, gifted Malik Kafur with twenty-three elephants. In return, the slave-general sent a 'khilat', a robe symbolic of Allauddin Khilji's overlordship over Prataparudra. And for the next few years, Prataparudra paid a heavy annual tribute to the sultan of Delhi.

But after a few years, Prataparudra fell back on his payments. This time, Allauddin Khilji sent another general, Khusrau Khan, to collect the payments. Khan arrived with the 'deadliest and the most advanced military technology anywhere in the world'. Circa 1318, after an intense battle, Prataparudra realised he was defeated. He agreed to 'cede to the Delhi Sultanate a single fortress, Badrakot, and deliver to Delhi, as an annual tribute, a substantial quantity of gold and jewels, 12,000 horses, and a hundred war elephants as large as demons'.[34]

Furthermore, as a sign of obeisance to Allauddin Khilji, Prataparudra 'ascended the eighteen steps leading up to the parapets of the citadel's stone wall. There, standing on top of the ramparts, in full view of both his fellow Telugu warriors and the invading northerners, the king turned his face in the direction of the imperial capital of Delhi. Bowing slowly, he kissed the rampart's surface in a gesture of humble submission.'[35] Prataparudra, once a mighty conqueror, was now a subordinate monarch. His public humiliation by a mere slave-general of the sultan of Delhi had cost him his credibility as a protector and sovereign. But his story does not end here.

In 1320, the Tughlaq dynasty usurped power by replacing

the Khilji dynasty. And in 1321, Delhi's new ruler, Sultan Ghiyasuddin Tughlaq, sent his son Ulugh Khan to collect arrears from Prataparudra. But after a six-month siege, Ulugh Khan could not breach the Kakatiya stone walls and retreated. Assuming victory, Prataparudra threw open the public granaries for a grand public feast. But such celebrations proved to be premature.

In 1323, Ulugh Khan returned to invade the Kakatiya capital with 63,000 mounted archers. This time, after holding the fort for five months, Prataparudra's forces surrendered. Upon breaching the walls, Ulugh Khan's forces annihilated Kakatiya warriors and 'subjected the capital to unchecked plunder and destruction'.[36] Prataparudra was captured on his elephant, his kingdom was annexed to the Tughlaq sultanate and he was sent to Delhi. According to most accounts, he died en route and the Kakatiya kingdom was extinguished.[37]

As soon as Ulugh Khan took charge, he destroyed the architectural marvels that represented the Kakatiya glory. The Kirti-thoranas, portals of glory that once represented the Kakatiya glory, were decimated. Beautiful sculptures and religious symbols that proclaimed the Kakatiya imperium were demolished.[38] Clearly, Ulugh Khan understood the importance of the symbolic power of politico-religious insignia. As Richard Eaton writes, it was 'a carefully calculated political act, designed as a means of decoupling a Hindu king's legitimate authority from his former kingdom'.[39]

Using material from the demolition, Ulugh Khan ordered the construction of a mosque. The mosque is now in ruins. The Tughlaqs also constructed another monument using salvaged material—an audience hall known as the Khush Mahal. It bears a striking resemblance to the hall of public audience (Diwane-aam) of Tughlakabad-Delhi. With the Kakatiya empire extinguished, the Tughlaqs turned the Deccan into a vassal state, appointed a governor, and renamed the Kakatiya capital as 'Sultanpur'. After the Kakatiya empire was vanquished by the Sultans of Delhi, chaos ensued.

However, fortunately, as the Rudreswara Temple—located in the original capital Anumakonda—is at a distance from Orugallu, the temple continues to exist even today. In 2007, the Archaeological Survey of India undertook the restoration of the Rudreswara temple to bring it back to its marvellous glory.[40] And, on 25 July 2021, UNESCO inscribed the Kakatiya Rudreswara temple as a UNESCO world heritage site.[41]

***

Temples are considered to be sanctuaries of the divine. Commonly, they are regarded as sacred spaces that connect humans to God. In precolonial society, temples, particularly in South India, were integral to weaving the social fabric of the society. As religious institutions, they played a significant role in prescribing the norms governing the society. They were also hubs of economic redistribution—conduits through which exchange occurred.

The story of the Rudreswara Temple—a 'crest jewel of Kakatiya art', which is interwoven with the rise and fall of the Kakatiya dynasty—helps understand how political sovereigns used temples to establish the legitimacy of their dynasty.[42] And today, it stands as 'a lone testimony to the highest level of creative, artistic and engineering talents' of the Kakatiya period, a monument that represents 'the golden era of Telugu language speaking people under the umbrella of Kakatiyan empire'.[43]

Notes

1 A.S. Altekar, 'The Rāshtrakūtas', in Ghulam Yazdani (ed.), *The Early History of the Deccan (Parts I-IV)*, Oxford University Press, 1960, pp. 315–468.
2 K.A. Nilakanta Sastri, 'The Cālukyas of Kalyāna', in R. S. Sharma (ed.), *A Comprehensive history of India: A.D. 985-1206 (Part 1)*, Indian History Congress/ People's Publishing House, 1957, pp. 72–102.
3 Cynthia Talbot, 'Political intermediaries in Kakatiya Andhra, 1175-1325', *The Indian Economic and Social History Review*, Sage, New Delhi/ Thousand Oaks, London, first published September 1994.
4 N.G. Ranga, *Kakatiya Nayaks: Their Contribution to Dakshinapathas Independence (1300-1370 A.D.)*, The Indian Peasants Institute, Nidubrolu, 1971, p. 15.
5 P.V. Sastry, N. Parabrahma, Ramesan (ed.), *The Kakatiyas of Warangal*, Government of Andhra Pradesh, Hyderabad, 1978, p. 30.
6 Richard M. Eaton, *India in the Persianate Age: 1000-1765*, Penguin, UK, 2019.
7 G. Yazdani, *The Early History Of The Deccan (Part VII-XI)*, Oxford University Press, Bombay, London, New York, 1960, pp. 585–97.
8 Ibid.
9 M. Rama Rao, 'Political History of The Kakatiyas: Rudra 1158 to 1195 AD', *Journal Of The Andhra Historical Research Society,* Vol. IV, July 1931, pp. 25–36.
10 Yazdani, op cit., pp. 585–97.
11 Abraham Early, *The First Spring: The Golden Age of India*, Penguin Books India, 2011, pp. 280–300.
12 J. Ramayya Pantulu, *Journal Of The Andhra Historical Research Society*, Vol. 4, Part 1 and 2, published by the Andhra Historical Research Society, Rajamundry, pp. 147–162.
13 N.G. Ranga, *Kakatiya Nayaks: Their Contribution to*

Dakshinapathas Independence (1300-1370 A.D.), The Indian Peasants Institute, Nidubrolu, 1971, pp. i–v.

14 Cynthia Talbot, *Precolonial India in Practice: Society, Region, and Identity in Medieval Andhra*, Oxford University Press, New York, 2001, pp. xiii, 305.

15 Ibid.

16 Bibhudutta Baral, Divyadarshan C.S. and Rakshitha, *Warangal Fort and Temple Architecture – Kakatiya Masterpiece*, published by Design Resource, NID, Bengaluru.

17 Marguerite Milward, *Artist in Unknown India*, published by T.W. Laurie, original from the University of California, 1948, pp. 62–5.

18 G.S.V. Suryanarayana Murthy, *Nomination Dossier for The Glorious Kakatiya Temples and Gateways, Rudreswara Temple,* Archaeological Survey of India, 2017, p. 19.

19 Zareena Parveen, 'An expansive treatise on the golden era of Kakatiyas', *The New Indian Express*, 31 August 2020, https://www.newindianexpress.com/lifestyle/books/2020/aug/31/an-expansive-treatise-on-the-golden-era-of-kakatiyas-2190481.html.

20 Suryanarayana Murthy, op cit., p. 19.

21 Ibid., p. 91.

22 Cited in Suryanarayana Murthy, op cit.

23 Ibid., p. 47.

24 Parveen, op cit.

25 Yazdani, op cit., pp. 374–458, 713.

26 Suryanarayana Murthy, op cit., p. 107.

27 Yazdani, op cit., p. 597.

28 Ibid.

29 Cynthia Talbot, 'Temples, Donors, and Gifts: Patterns of Patronage in Thirteenth-Century South India', *The Journal of Asian Studies*, Vol. 50, No. 2, published by Association for Asian Studies, May 1991, pp. 308–340.

30 Richard M. Eaton, *A Social History of the Deccan, 1300-1761:*

Eight Indian Lives, Part 1, Vol. 8, Cambridge University Press, 2005, p. 17.

31 B. Satyanarayana Singh, *The Art and Architecture of The Kakatiyas,* Bharatiya Kala Prakashan, 1999, pp. 33–65.

32 Quoted in *The New Cambridge History of India*, Vol. 1, Part 8, Richard Eaton, Cambridge University Press, 2008, p. 9.

33 Richard M. Eaton, op cit., pp. 9–32.

34 Ibid.

35 Ibid.

36 Ibid.

37 Cynthia Talbot, op cit., p. 176.

38 Phillip B. Wagoner, 'The Place of Warangal's Kirti-Toranas in the History of Indian Islamic Architecture', *Religion and the Arts, a Journal from Boston College*, No. 1 (2004), pp. 6–36.

39 Richard M. Eaton, 'Temple Desecration And Indo-Muslim States', *Journal of Islamic Studies*, Vol. 11, No. 3 (September 2000), pp. 283-319.

40 Amarnath K. Menon, 'ASI takes up restoration work at Rudraeswara Swamy temple', *India Today*, 15 January 2007, https://www.indiatoday.in/magazine/heritage/story/20070115-archaeological-survey-of-india-is-doing-the-restoration-and-coversation-of-rudraeswara-swamy-temple-andhra-pradesh-749319-2007-01-15.

41 Saurabh Sharma, '800-years-old Rudreswara (Ramappa) Temple is now a world heritage site. Know its history', *Mint*, 25 July 2021 https://www.livemint.com/news/india/800yearsold-rudreswara-ramappa-temple-is-now-a-world-heritage-site-know-its-history-11627228653957.html.

42 Suryanarayana Murthy, op cit., p. 64.

43 Ibid.

The Womb of the Earth

Siddhartha Sarma

Nilachal Hill in Guwahati rises about 560 feet from its surroundings and casts a vast shadow to the south and east in the evening. At dawn, seen from the middle of the Brahmaputra to its north, the hill appears like a citadel stretching interminably along the riverbank. On one of its summits, the most significant Mother Goddess temple in the subcontinent has cast an even larger influence over devotees. Kamakhya is at once a fertility goddess and an anchor of tantric beliefs. Mahamaya, as one of the many names her devotees use to address her—the goddess of illusion and deep magic, appeased with blood sacrifice. Yet she is also a manifestation of formidable creative forces and the recipient of a diverse range of contemplational and devotional rituals, worship and practices. But in considering the complex ideas of sacred geography, scriptures, rituals and personal faith that surround her, the exceptional nature of the goddess and her temple often passes unremarked.

Towards the end of his life, the Axomiya polymath Banikanta Kakati addressed this puzzle: the temple notwithstanding, Shakti worship is actually uncommon in the Brahmaputra Valley, and has historically been so. It is true that, through the usual osmosis of beliefs caused by the presence of a major pilgrimage site and more recent cultural influences, there are exclusively goddess worshippers in Lower or Western Assam, particularly among the upper castes. But they are far outnumbered by Shaivites and Vaishnavites. In his own time, Kakati knew there were more Shiva temples in the region than that of any other deity, while the egalitarian, idol-rejecting Vaishnavism of the great medieval scholar Sankaradeva has a deep cultural presence that has shaped Axomiya self-identity, literature and music far more than any other religious tradition has. Kamakhya's existence in the valley, and its enduring importance within Hinduism, is therefore exceptional in the Axomiya context.

In 1948, Kakati published *The Mother Goddess Kamakhya*, which pieces together the story of a temple and the inferred political processes that willed it into existence.

He found the beginnings of the explanation in the *Kalika Purana*, one of the minor Puranas, most of it composed in Assam sometime before the eleventh century CE. A Shakta scripture, its philosophical ambitions are rather modest, but it attempts to bring together the major Hindu goddesses into a cohesive singularity around the idea of Kamakhya. And it has this story.

A man named Naraka from Mithila led an expedition to colonise what was then the 'anarya' Brahmaputra Valley, whose original inhabitants (called Kiratas by Puranic Hindus; an umbrella term for the many native tribes of eastern India and the lower Himalayas) worshipped a form of Shiva. Naraka's religious guide—the text says this was Vishnu himself—told him to settle Brahmins in the valley, promote the worship of the Goddess Kamakhya and deny patronage to other gods, including Shiva. The Kiratas withdrew to the 'eastern sea' and Shaivism went underground.

But it lingered, and the Shaivite remnants decided to bring the settlers' leader over to their side. Bana, ruler of a neighbouring kingdom and a formidable Shaivite, struck up friendship with Naraka and influenced him to abandon both goddess worship and patronage of dwijas (literally, twice-born, i.e. 'upper' castes). Palace politics followed, and the story then introduces the familiar narrative device of an upset ascetic's curse (in this case, the sage Vashistha). Naraka is finally slain by Vishnu in the form of Krishna. In his last moments, the fallen hero from Mithila sees Kamakhya on the battlefield, fighting in the form of Kali by the side of Krishna.

Naraka, the figure if not precisely this version of him, appears in numerous texts, including some of the later strands of the Mahabharata. In his afterlife he has found some kind of endurance—the mighty hill range south of Nilachal is named after him and has traditionally been accorded occult significance by tantric adepts. At least three major dynasties in medieval Assam claimed descent from him. For most Indians, he would be familiar for lending his name to Naraka Chaturdashi, the second day of Diwali, commemorating the night when the man, given asuric characteristics by various scriptures, made his last stand in his fortress against his disavowed deities. Medieval scriptures have rather drastic solutions for apostasy, particularly when the apostate is a fallen hero and an oath-breaker.

Here the wronged god is Vishnu, indicating the composers of the *Kalika Purana* had Vaishnavite sympathies or were writing for a monarch who did. The Shaivite version of Kamakhya's foundational story is the better-known episode, found in several puranic iterations, involving the self-immolation of the Goddess Sati, and Shiva's tandava.

Sati, wife of Shiva, was outraged when her father, King Daksha, held a great sacrifice but did not invite them. Confronting her father, and humiliated by him, she immolated herself in the sacrificial fire.

Shiva then picked up her body and began his dance of destruction. With the whole of creation in peril, the gods asked Vishnu to intervene, and the divine Sudarshan discus cut Sati's body into several pieces. The places on earth where these fell became Shakti Peethas, of which eighteen are major Mother Goddess pilgrimage sites. Sati's yoni fell at the site of Kamakhya, becoming the foremost Shakti Peetha.

Through such layers of myth, minor puranas like *Kalika* provide clues for larger historical and political processes. In Naraka's story we catch a glimpse of large-scale events witnessed elsewhere in the subcontinent's many peripheries: settlement from Aryavarta, the conflation of indigenous belief systems with emerging ideas of Shaivism, the denial of patronage to Brahmins and official deities leading to conflict among settler factions, and finally, the triumphant return of dwija-sanctioned religious practices, although only in the limited geography of Pragjyotishpura, capital city of the Kamarupa kingdom in myth and eventually, recorded history.

After ablutions at the Saubhagya Kund, the rectangular lake adjoining the temple, the devotee today has to proceed in a serpentine queue around the structure before entering through a door in the northern face of the mandapa, a square hall. West of the mandapa is the nritya mandapa, its sides twice in length to that of the mandapa. And on the distant side of the nritya mandapa is the last hall, the bhoga mandapa, all connected in sequence by doors.

The mandapa has two entrances, one each on the north and south, while there is another on the western, apsidal face of the nritya mandapa, originally intended to be the main entrance.

In recent decades, this portal has been gradually not used for entrance of devotees, although exceptions are made for the mighty in the land. In this too there is a continuum with medieval practices, where proximity to the divine was determined by lineage and social position. The ordinary devotee therefore finds themself deposited directly in the mandapa through its northern, smaller door, which now has a porch-like extension of later construction. Inside the mandapa, they circumambulate around a central idol and can offer prayers to deities and demi-gods in niches on the walls of the chamber.

On the eastern wall of the mandapa is another portal with stone steps leading down into what is, literally in the case of Kamakhya, the garbha griha. A perennial spring, fed by deep aquifers, emerges from the bedrock of the hill. At the convergence of two massive rocks is a fissure in the approximate shape of a vulva, with a uniform depth of ten inches.

The association of goddess worship with this site is older than the beginnings of temple construction in the subcontinent, and the summit of Nilachal Hill has several such yoni fissures, all of which became garbha grihas for temples of goddesses which together form part of the Kamakhya complex.

The *Kalika Purana* has yet another clue for those seeking to understand the evolution of sacred geography. Naraka did not bring Kamakhya worship with him from Mithila. Rather, it already existed at the site, and Kamakhya was a traditional Kirata goddess. Some texts even imply that Naraka himself was a Kirata warlord co-opted by the newcomers. In the period immediately before the emergence of Pragjyotishpura as a historical city in the fifth century CE and the arrival of settlers from Aryavarta, the area that is Guwahati today was inhabited by Khasis and Garos. The Khasis had a creator goddess of extraordinary power named Ka-Mei-Kha, and the site of the temple complex was her sacrificial ground of considerable significance for them. The composers of the *Kalika Purana* did not know of this but were aware that the traditions they were drawing on, and the sacredness of the yoni fissure, were much older than the transplanted belief systems of Hinduism, which even then were in the process of coalescing.

By the beginning of the second millennium CE, Kamakhya was an established goddess for Hindus, her origin myth having been accommodated in canonical scriptures through the story of Sati and her marriage to Shiva. This process is similar to how Manasa, a tribal goddess of healing and protection against snakes, was accommodated in the Hindu hierarchy of deities by being declared the daughter of Shiva and therefore subsidiary to him.

A stone temple existed at the site by this period, but its date of construction, or the king who ordered this, is not known. This is a striking anomaly, because we do know of kings in the valley before the Ahom kingdom, and about their major construction projects. But of the temple, there is no claimant.

Therefore, the irony that in trying to date the earliest known period of existence of the temple to the mid-ninth century, we must compare the earliest parts of the temple that have survived with similar ruins in historical Tezpur, the mythical capital of King Bana, who engineered Naraka's downfall.

By the beginning of the sixteenth century, there were no more claimants to descent from Naraka. The world had become all too real, and dynastic survival more perilous than it had ever been. The Muslim rulers of Bengal had been trying to invade the valley for two hundred years. In the valley there were two claimants to greatness. In the west was Koch king Biswa Singha, who had united the tribes of western Assam into the Kamata kingdom, with its capital a short distance from modern Cooch Behar. In eastern Assam, the Ahoms had begun expanding and consolidating their rule. For decades the balance of power swung between these three players.

In one such tumultuous year, Biswa Singha made the journey up Nilachal and arrived at Kamakhya.

The venerable old temple had suffered damage, either at human hands or owing to natural calamities. The earthquakes that periodically pass through the Northeast have levelled monumental architecture in a more definitive manner than the most dedicated iconoclast. On the other hand, an invasion by the Bengal nawab, Husein Shah, had occurred in the closing years of the fifteenth century and could have also been to blame. The stone temple was repaired and worship resumed.

In 1564 another army from Bengal arrived at Nilachal. It was led, or so the sources claim, by Kalapahar, a Hindu lately converted to Islam and a zealous iconoclast who had sacked Konark and attacked the Jagannath Temple complex in Puri. Biswa Singha's renovations did not survive.

The Koch kingdom did, however, and rule had passed to the greatest king of that dynasty, Naranarayan (reigned 1540–87). He visited the ruined temple and directed its reconstruction.

The person ultimately entrusted with the project, Megha Mukdam, completed it within a year.

There were practical problems. The restoration of the original stone pinnacle turned out to be more difficult than anticipated. Megha Mukdam's masons therefore built the shikhara of brick, surmounting the stone base and lower sections of the walls, which were all that remained of the original temple.

The three outer chambers acquired a distinct, different roof, in the form of a barrel vault, a design which the locals call 'tortoise-backed', and students of Indian temple architecture would recognise as 'hastipristha'. Although these design choices and stylistic combinations became remarkably influential in the construction of other temples in the valley, giving rise to what is called Nilachal architecture, the barrel vault is of a much more venerable and unexpected lineage. Its original template can be found in the Parasurameshwara Temple in Bhubaneshwar, dating to the middle of the eighth century CE. Through a circuitous route, one of the oldest surviving elements of temple architecture in eastern India had made its way to Kamakhya through construction projects in Bengal. Thus both iconoclasm and architecture, vandalism and construction run as common threads through Bengal, Assam and Odisha during this period. Coincidentally, this type of barrel vault is also resilient to seismic stresses, as the later history of Assam shows.

Nor were these influences the only imports from the west. Of the many priestly families which live in the temple complex today, several are Parbatiya Gosains, descended from a renowned Shakta seer of Bengal who was invited and given stewardship of the temple by Ahom king Siba Singha in the eighteenth century.

A hundred and twenty years after it was rebuilt, Megha

Mukdam's brick-and-stone temple still stood, but the valley was on the brink of devastation.

The Koch kingdom had fragmented into two, and the contestants were now the Mughals and the Ahoms. In 1671, the Ahoms defeated the Mughals on the river next to Nilachal and recaptured the temple complex. Despite its excellent strategic location, the hilltop had never been fortified, with the Ahom fort located at Itakhuli, upstream, where downtown Guwahati begins today. The victorious Ahoms found the temple complex desecrated, although not with the finality shown by earlier invaders.

At that moment, in the culmination of a definitive war to determine Assam's sovereignty, the Ahoms could have chosen to leave their imprimatur on the temple in a comprehensive manner. They did have the resources and talent for this. Ahom monumental architecture had acquired definite forms by then and can be seen in some remarkable examples in Upper Assam from the turn of that century.

However, the Ahoms chose a major repair project instead, restoring some damaged sculptures and the newer shikhara and barrel vault, as well as the massive walls and two gates which surround the temple. In doing this they ignored the temptation, to which even modern governments are known to succumb, of leaving political legacies through temple reconstruction. Perhaps they recognised that, in its essence, Kamakhya is about what lies in the garbha griha, and not in the mutable structure which encloses it.

The visitor today will find the clearest iteration of Ahom architecture in the doors of the nritya mandapa, while in its form and structure, the temple remains what Megha Mukdam had intended it to be.

The shikhara admits no light. There are no gaps or even loopholes in the plinth or walls, nor are there any windows or skylights, however modest, on the roof over the garbha griha. Descending about 6 feet from the entrance of the garbha griha, the devotee is enveloped in an amniotic darkness, facing the opening in the rock while enclosed by the towering vault of the shikhara. The effect can be described as an approximation of a womb, which may not be coincidental. In this, the physical core of Kamakhya, one may finally understand why, of all the major sects of Hinduism as practiced today, the sacred geography of Shakti worship is the most rooted in the natural features of the site rather than in the architectural features of the temple.

This sense of enclosure continues in the three outer chambers, particularly the nritya mandapa, which in most medieval north Indian temples is a pillared space without walls. But in the Kamakhya Temple, each succeeding chamber is darker than the preceding one, culminating in the garbha griha.

Kamakhya is therefore built on two levels, the higher comprising the three outer chambers, and the lower comprising the garbha griha. The earliest temple builders seem to have chosen this plan, partly because excavating the area near the garbha griha to make the foundations level with it would have meant chipping away at the rock layer from which the stream emerges.

Outside the temple, one can approach a paved circumambulation route or pradakshinapatha which is approximately 8 feet lower than the surrounding courtyard and level with the foundation blocks. This route is surrounded by a wall which has striking and stylised figures of ganas inlaid on it.

In the course of the outer circumambulation, one can see the base of the temple, which makes about half the height of the structure. The base of the garbha griha has sixteen sides and consists of five layers of stone mouldings, one atop the other. Their design creates deep horizontal shadows between each layer. The mouldings are each designed differently. The lowest has almost no decorations, but a guide familiar with the foundations can show the visitor where the stones have been deeply sliced in the shape of lotus petals. The overall resemblance is to gigantic claws digging into the earth, anchoring the mass of the temple. Each succeeding layer of the foundation is decorated with more sophistication than its lower counterpart. The reliefs carved on the topmost and widest layer are striking in their sculptural precision. On this level are carved the sixty-four yoginis which form a key part of goddess worship and Shakti temple architecture. The other figures to be found at the same level on a circumambulation of the outer walls are bhairavas, forms of deities associated with Shaivism. The other place where bhairavas occur are high up on the outer walls of the garbha griha.

The rebuilt shikhara is architecturally distinct from most north Indian temples, being neither a dome like those found in medieval temples of Gujarat and Rajasthan, nor curvilinear in the Nagara style, but somewhere in between, resembling the shikhara of the Kalighat temple in Kolkata. The twenty projecting bands which comprise the shikhara converge at the top and are surmounted by three amalakas. Here, too, the amalakas are not spherical as is traditional in north Indian architecture, but sculpted as lotuses in bloom, one placed atop and facing the other. On the topmost and smallest amalaka is a trident, the symbol of the goddess in this case. Between the shikhara and the barrel vault are several smaller shikharas over the mandapa, which also is an innovation to be found in the Nilachal school of temple architecture.

The sculptural details on the main shikhara will be hidden from the devotee circumambulating along the ancient stone foundation layers of the temple. Instead, their parikrama will bring them to two halls supported by brick pillars adjoining the main temple. Both halls are of much later construction, but on occasional pillars one may find, mounted, beautiful reliefs which once belonged on the walls and subsidiary structures of the earliest temple. One of the halls was originally intended as a market for icons of the goddess and the necessary offerings that devotees sought to carry inside the temple with them. The other hall is meant for animal sacrifice.

It is customary for devotees to offer sacrificial chickens, pigeons, goats and buffaloes and less commonly, ducks to the goddess. Animal sacrifice has been traditionally associated with Devi worship in the subcontinent. While there are occasional controversies about this, the practice at Kamakhya is largely undertaken today in much the same manner as it would have been in the late medieval period.

Human sacrifice is a much more problematic legacy. There is some evidence that it was practised at the temple in medieval times and at least till the earliest part of the colonial period, but not predominantly so. Stronger associations can be found in farther corners of the region, in places over which the last tides of Hinduism washed. A little more than 550 kilometres east of Guwahati, on the outskirts of the town of Sadiya, was the fourteenth century temple of Tamreshwari, after the beautiful roof made of beaten tamra or copper, where an aspect of Kali was worshipped. It was more popular among

Axomiya, Deori and other communities as Kesa Khaiti, or the 'goddess who eats raw meat', because this was offered as prasad there. Along its western wall was a designated place for human sacrifice. The original temple no longer exists, being submerged by a nearby river in the 1950s, and the current temple nearby has less objectionable sacrifices and practices.

The occult and tantric, however, are integral aspects of Kamakhya and all the other goddess temples in the complex atop Nilachal. Adepts and novices journey from far corners of India, particularly during the Axomiya month of Ahaar, in the middle of June. This is the time of the Ambubachi Mela, when the temple is closed for three days because the goddess menstruates. On the fourth day, worship resumes. One may find the occasional tantric adept camped on the temple grounds during the entire month, and families of Shaktas as well. Of the approximately four million visitors to the temple each year, a substantial number, particularly the more distant ones, arrive during Ambubachi, some at the culmination of a countrywide pilgrimage of the major Shakti Peethas.

Devi worship, in its doctrines, rituals, scriptures and practices, covers a diverse range of faith-based positions, from the everyday worship of lay believers to the rigorous observances and arcana of tantric adepts. Its roots go far back in time to layers of indigenous and folk beliefs which have since been given formality while being subsumed by caste Hindu belief systems, even as the original believers were pushed to the 'eastern sea' of the mainstream mindspace. These rooted positions have proven curiously resistant to change and the influence of reformist tendencies, just as the ancient sites of this worship anchor and outlast the physical structures that have been built and rebuilt over them. But in its strong bonds to the earth, to the vitality of natural processes, and even to the idea of blood sacrifice, through parallel symbolisms of water and blood, creation and death, goddess worship touches some of the more primeval and atavistic chords in the network of religious ideas that together comprise what is called Hinduism. Kamakhya represents these extraordinarily vital bonds in many unique ways.

Vithoba of Pandharpur: One with the Lord

Neelesh Kulkarni

'It is not Vaikuntha I want—I don't want to go to heaven. Even if you wanted to give me the kingdom of Indra, I still wouldn't want it, oh Pandurang,' said Namdev, as he clung to the lotus feet of Vithal.

'I want to lie forever at the entrance to your abode here in Pandharpur where every bhakta going for your darshan will walk over my body before going in. If the dust from the feet of those that come to worship you falls on my body, I shall be in heaven itself,' he begged of the Lord.

'Tatashtu (so be it),' said Vithal, and the first stair of the temple split open, Namdev dived into the crevice, and just as it closed up again, all the other members of his family plunged in too. The earth joined up again, and it was as if it had never parted. This happened in CE 1346, and from then, the first step in the stairs that lead up to the main Pandurang temple is known as the Namdevpayari (payari meaning step in Marathi). All worshippers going into the temple carefully avoid stepping on to it and bow to the saint before going in.

I stand at the shrine to Namdev on the payari in the main square at the entrance of the Shree Vithal Rukmini Devasthan.

A brass idol of Namdev is placed on the stair every morning and then taken away at night. Devotees who go into the temple stop to bow to it before walking in. I touch my forehead to the idol of the saint. Instead of stepping over it, I step back and let my eyes wander over the temple of Maharashtra's most revered and popular deity, to which I was returning after almost thirty years.

My earliest memories of Pandharpur and going to the Vithal temple are walking through narrow cobbled streets with my cousins and watching my step to ensure I did not stumble on one of the cobblestones which jutted out from the surface. All this has changed, and my cab driver takes me through some fairly broad, though still considerably crowded, streets which end at the main temple square. My cousin, Vaishali Bidkar, a local who is accompanying me, tells me that the road widening was done in 1982 when a determined administration demolished several residences and shops flanking the narrow streets to make way for the devotees.

Having been driven 210 kms from Pune over almost four hours, I am glad that I can get down at the temple gate and do not have to walk further. Vaishali, however, complains that it has destroyed homes and shops and some of the historical landmarks and archaeological markers.

However, my eyes are busy taking in the temple. We walk around it, taking in the fortified walls and the nine entry gates, the shops selling prasad and the people milling around each entrance. Having soaked in the atmosphere and having circumambulated the temple, we prepare to enter the holiest and most revered spots in Maharashtra where Krishna as Vithal or Pandurang has stood for over 5,000 years to honour a word given to a devotee.

As the legend goes, Krishna came to Dindirvana looking for Rukmini, his queen who had left Dwarka in a huff, angered by his overindulgence of Satyabhama, his other wife. Unable to bear her absence, Krishna came looking for her, but she refused to recognise him as he appeared before her as a cowherd. As he turned to go back to Dwarka, he thought of paying a visit to his devotee Pundarik (or Pundalik in Marathi), who sat in his tiny hut by the river Chandrabhaga, rubbing the feet of his parents. Pundarik was surprised to see his humble abode suddenly light up and, turning, saw the Lord himself appear before him. Considering his duty towards his parents to be above his devotion to the Lord, he casually threw a brick and asked the Lord to wait while he finished.

Here the stories differ; while some say that after he finished, he ran and drowned himself so that the Lord would not go back, others say he begged forgiveness of the Lord and asked him to stay back. Whatever is true, till date, his name is taken with that of the Lord, and the salutation to Vithal is '*Bola Pundalikvarade Hari Vithal—Shree Dnyandeva Tukaram*' (Take the name of Vithal who gave a boon to Pundalik, followed by the names of two other ardent devotees, Dnyandev and Tukaram). Vithal has also stayed back in Pandharpur, standing on the very same brick with his hands on his hips.

The legend of Pundalik is supposedly 5,000 years old, and references to the deity and Pandharpur are found in both the *Padma Purana* and the *Skanda Purana*. These mention Shiva himself telling both Parvati and Narada that a glimpse of Vithal at Pandharpur was as pious as sixty thousand years of penance.

Though the locals say that the Lord created Pandharpur before he created Vaikuntha, his abode (which might explain the erstwhile narrow lanes), the first mention of the temple in recorded history is somewhere in the second century CE.

In his epic Marathi poem, *Malu Taran*, Malu Sonar mentions that King Shalivahana of the Satavahana dynasty got this temple repaired, thus putting its existence at certainly more than 2,000 years. Additionally, there are references to the temple on fifth century stone tablets discovered near the site during recent excavations. Similarly, Adi Shankaracharya,who came to Pandharpur somewhere at the beginning of the ninth century, also wrote about it. The Hoysala kings in the eleventh century considerably added to the temple and Hemadri Pandit, the prime minister of King Ramachandra Yadav of Devgiri, expanded it substantially towards the mid-thirteenth century.

This explains the many architectural styles present in the temple I see before me. The entry gate and the areas inside it are in the Hoysala style and probably the oldest standing structures. The sanctum santorum is Hemadpanthi—the rugged style using stone and lime, popularised by Hemadri Pandit. The sabhamandap, located just above the entrance staircase, was probably added in parts in the seventeenth century in either Shivaji or Shahu Maharaj's time when extensive renovations were carried out and a part was added some sixty-five years back.

I am standing in front of the Darshanbari, just across the temple gate, and only a few years old. It is a six-storey building in which one floor has amenities, and the other five have steel pipes creating corridors along which devotees walk up and then down before entering the main gate. Before this building came up, queues for darshan extended for kilometres, but these now move vertically through the bari.

Right in front of the Darshanbari is the samadhi of Sant Chokha Mela, who lived in the fourteenth century and was not allowed into the temple as he was a 'lower' caste. The spot where the samadhi is located was where he would sit all day singing praises to the Lord, and the story goes that he could actually see the idol of Vithal from there. This seems impossible to me since the idol is now some 700 feet away, and even if there were no buildings in between then, seeing the Lord clearly at this distance would have been impossible. I ask Vaishali's husband, Vasant Rao, about this, and he points to a circular platform just above the stairs and tells me this was where the idol initially was and when they shifted it back, they let the platform be. He says that the idol was probably shifted back after it was brought back from Anegundi, near Hampi, the capital of the Vijayanagara empire.

In 1337, Krishnadeva Raya of Vijayanagara came to Pandharpur and was so in awe of the idol that he wanted to relocate the idol to the capital of his empire. As the story goes, Vithal appeared in the dreams of Krishnadeva Raya and said he could come with the king provided his devotees could have unfettered access to him in his capital too. Krishnadeva Raya agreed, and the idol was shifted to the Vijaya Vittala temple in Hampi. There the idol was decked with ornaments of gold studded with pearls and diamonds and became the royal families' deity with hardly any access for the common folk. In Pandharpur, on the other hand, Vithal's devotees were distraught; their life seemed incomplete without their Lord. Then Bhanudas, an ardent devotee, promised to bring him back and set out for Vijayanagara.

When he reached the Vijaya Vittala temple, all the guards fell asleep and the locks to the temple opened by themselves, and as Bhanudas walked in, Vithal appeared before him and asked him to take him back.

'How shall I carry you, my Lord?' asked Bhanudas. 'I have neither horse nor carriage.'

In reply, the Lord shrunk in size, and Bhanudas carried him on his shoulders back to Pandharpur, where he was joyfully welcomed and re-established in his temple, where he grew back to his original size. All was well again!

Almost all the signage in the temple is in both Marathi and Kannada, bringing home the Karnataka connection vividly to me. The famous song 'Kanda Vithalatujhyadaree aalo' (Oh Vithal from Karnataka, I have come to your door) floats from a radio in the sweetshop nearby, and I begin to hum it as we move into the temple.

'Pandurang Hari, Pandurang Hari,' we chant as we move up and down the Darshanbari floors to approach the entrance gate.

The name 'Pandurang', another name for Vithal, is also of Kannada origin, and some stone tablets dating to the thirteenth century excavated near the western gate indicate this. The Shaivites dispute this and say that the word Pandurang comes from the Marathi words 'pandhara' meaning white and 'rang', meaning complexion. As Shiva is portrayed as very fair in mythology, they claimed that Vithal was Shiva. However, the Vaishnavites contest this argument and say that Vithal was Krishna whose body had turned white due to the dust from the hooves of the cows he was herding, having settled on it. This debate often turned acrimonious, and many were the attempts made to unite both factions, giving rise to many myths, such as the one of Narhari Sonar.

Narhari Sonar was the most noted goldsmith of the area, but when he was called forth to craft a crown for Vithal, he flatly refused.

'Vithal is Krishna, and I am a worshipper of Shiva. I cannot set sight on Vithal,' he said.

On being persuaded, he agreed to craft the crown but said he would take the measurements for the crown blindfolded, and then make the crown according to them. His condition being accepted, he was escorted into the sanctum santorum blindfolded, as he desired. He made an exquisite crown that did not fit when set upon the Lord's head. Narhari was stunned; it had never happened before! He set out on a second blindfolded mission with the same disastrous results, and the third that followed was no better. The fourth time, in pure frustration, he tore the blindfold away and saw none but Shiva in front of him and saw him dissolve into Vithal. The blindfold on his mind disappeared too, and he became one of the most ardent devotees of Vithal.

In the fourteenth century, Sant Dnyaneshwar (called Gynaneshwar in Hindi) first came here with his followers. He settled the differences between the two factions by stating that Vithal was Krishna, but he carried a Shiva lingam carved on his crown.

He also bade his followers walk to Pandharpur twice a year in the Ashadh and Kartik months of the Hindu calendar, reaching on ekadashi or the eleventh day of the lunar calendar. The practice, called vaari, has continued unabated for over seven hundred years. The number of people walking from the samadhis of Dnyaneshwar at Alandi and Tukaram at Dehu, both near Pune, is now the single biggest exodus of humans from one place to another conducted so regularly. Upwards of one and a half million people walk the path twice a year now, in perfect peace and harmony, singing, dancing and chanting the name of the Lord. They come from differing social backgrounds and are from all age brackets. Often, the younger age group also includes many software engineers and corporate executives. They walk in self-contained groups, each called a 'dindi'. Every dindi has a leader; there is a group to look after accommodation, one for food and one also includes musicians and singers who chant the name of the Lord. The order in which they walk is predetermined, and there is never any dispute or rowdyism. Their discipline can be gauged from the fact that there are often only a few hundred policemen to monitor over one million plus people.

The Vaarkari sampraday, or the community of those undertaking the vaari, is probably the most egalitarian community in the spiritual firmament of the country, with all castes represented in it. No one in the vaari is a brahmin or a lower caste—each one is just a varkari.

The phalanx of saints associated with the worship of Vithal has come from all communities. Namdev was a tailor, Dnyaneshwar a Brahmin, Tukaram a Baniya, Chokha Mela, a Mahar or lower caste, Narhari Das a goldsmith. Even women saints abound with Janabai and Kanhoptara, who was a prostitute, being amongst them.

Stories are aplenty of how Vithal donned the garb of an ordinary person to help these saints. Janabai, it is said, was overloaded with housework by her in-laws and so she would not find time to take the name of Vithal. So the Lord would take a human form every day and go and wash her clothes for her. Since Chokha Mela was of a lower caste, the Brahmins would not allow him inside the temple or let him partake of the prasad. Vithal would, it is said, go to Chokha Mela's hut every day and eat with him. Once, when he spilt some curd on his garment, the Brahmins in the temple were surprised to find the curd on the attire of the idol.

The prevalence of these stories ensures that Vithal is, to his devotees, not a distant God but a friend and companion who is also a loved equal. The personalisation of the Lord is clear from the name he is addressed by in the local dialect—he is called Vithoba, which is quite akin to a Samuel being called Sam or a Debendranath being called Debu in his family. His consort Rukmini is similarly addressed as Rukumai or Mother Rukmini. Strangely, Vithal is also called Mauli or a loving mother, probably to indicate the closeness one feels with the mother. Vithal is to his devotees a God who is a part of their families.

This personalisation of the Lord came home to me the very first time I came to Pandharpur with my grandfather, more than fifty years ago, when I was about twelve. He was a varkari (one who walks in the vaari) and had all his life walked the vaari twice a year. A prosperous farmer and head of a large village, he would for those twenty days turn into a mendicant and carrying his ektara (a single-stringed instrument), walk with the dindi, singing the praises of the Lord. He would sleep on the ground and eat whatever was available. I joined him for the last day's walk that particular year. Part of a huge crowd, we jostled for space and with great difficulty entered Pandharpur, but as we came close to the temple, he stopped, looked at the dome of the temple and folding his hands, muttered a prayer and turned back to return. I was stunned!

'Didn't you want to meet the Lord?' I asked him.

'Yes,' he replied.

'But then why are we not going into the temple?' I asked him.

'He knows I came; I don't have to show him my face to establish that,' he replied.

As far as he was concerned, he had done his duty, his karma, and by bowing to the temple, had informed the Lord that he had come—nothing further was necessary. To him, his Vithal had been waiting for him, keeping a lookout for him, and when he folded his hands, Vithal looked at him, acknowledged his presence, and told him he was free to go back.

Thinking of my grandfather, I step over the Namdev payari and reach a small porch, move through the narrow corridor bowing to the Ganesh idol on the left, step into the sabha mandap. The sabha mandap or congregation hall is where pilgrims gather before entering the sanctum santorum. Right in front are two deep stambhas—tapering pillars—going right up to the roof with niches cut into them to enable the placing of earthen lamps to light up the temple. Their presence is a rather strange feature since these are generally in the outer courtyard of every temple and never inside the sabha mandap or any built-up structure. Pandit Haridas Badve, who has joined us at the behest of my cousin, explains that this was so, as this area was an open courtyard and was subsequently enclosed. Moving ahead from there, we come across a small temple to Garuda and then the Hanuman idol consecrated by Swami Ramdas, the spiritual guru of Shivaji.

Ramdas Swami, also referred to as Samarth (meaning strong or capable), was reluctant to visit the temple as he was a Rama bhakta and could not imagine worshipping anyone but Rama. When being persuaded by some of his disciples, he did enter it, Vithal appeared before him as Rama. Seeing Rama, Ramdas Swami thought it appropriate that an idol of Hanuman also be part of the temple and consecrated this idol sometime in the mid-seventeenth century.

Moving further down, we exit the sabha mandap and,

going past the idols of Jaya and Vijaya, the doorkeepers of Lord Vishnu, step into the smaller 'solahkhambi' hall which is the darshan mandap. Of the sixteen pillars (solahkhambi), four are silver-plated, and each of them has detailed images of gods and goddesses carved on them. Pandit Haridas points to the sculpture of a hunter carrying a gun carved on one of them and uses that to theorise that this hall was built a little over two hundred years ago by one Shenvi from a village called Daud. He explains that the original temple was probably only the garbhagriha or sanctum santorum. We ask him about the ruins found near the Namdev payari. He corrects himself to say that the garbhagriha was the oldest standing structure and probably added on in the era of Hemadri Pant. He adds that the idol was perhaps consecrated here after Bhanudas brought it back from Vijayanagara.

Of the sixteen pillars, one is called the Garuda stambha or the pillar of Garuda, the eagle on whom Vishnu rides. We move to it and embrace the pillar, as is the custom, seeking the permission of the mount and companion to go in and meet the Lord.

Badve shows us a stone tablet fixed in the wall of the mandap against which people rub their backs before going in to meet the Lord. The tablet has a list of eighty-four donors to the temple in the twelfth century, and devotees believe that rubbing their back against the same relieves one of the sins accumulated over a lifetime. We cleanse ourselves too and enter the garbhagriha through silver-plated gates, and there right before me under a canopy supported on pillars of pure silver stands the Lord, his feet firmly planted on a brick, his hands on his hips. I am overwhelmed and bow down and murmur, 'Vithal, Vithal, Vithal.'

The idol, made of black stone, is 3 feet and 9 inches high, and is dressed in a dhoti and upper garment, both made of silk. Ornaments studded with precious stones adorn the body, and a conical crown of gold sits lightly on his forehead. I cannot locate the Shivalingam carved on it, but Haridas tells me the crown itself is in the shape of a lingam, and hence Vithal is carrying the symbol of Shiva (the lingam) on his forehead.

The ritual worship of the Lord starts at 4 a.m. with the 'kakadaarti' or prayer to wake up the Lord, followed by the 'panchamritsnana' or bath with the 5 nectars (a mixture of cow milk, clarified butter, curd, honey and jaggery). At noon, the priests wash his feet, anoint the Lord with essence, conduct the aarti and then offer him the afternoon meal. The food is cooked in the temple kitchen and brought to the Lord on a silver plate 30 inches in diameter. The offering is then distributed amongst the officiating priests as prasad. There are 2 more rounds of aarti before the aarti in the late afternoon and the evening. Shejaarti, the aarti to bid the Lord sleep, is at 11 p.m., after which the priests take the sandals of the Lord to his bed-chamber, which is just off the garbhagriha. Another round of 5 aartis follows this, and the temple is then closed for the day.

The mahapuja is the most significant event for devotees, and it started during the reign of the Peshwas. It was initially a puja in which only the king, the peshwa or the nobles participated. The priests subsequently opened this up to paying members of the public though even now, on all-important occasions, the chief minister of Maharashtra performs the first mahapuja.

When I was a teenager, my family offered such a puja to thank the Lord for my father getting promoted at work. I recollect getting up at 3 a.m. and, after bathing, dressing in new clothes, going through the south gate at 4 a.m. to enter the sanctum santorum directly. The puja lasted a total of two hours, and I was allowed to wash the feet of the Lord as the priests chanted mantras. The proximity to the Lord and the atmosphere created by the chanting has stayed with me to date.

Haridas tell us that the practice has now been stopped because the feet of the idol were getting eroded by the constant touch. This is now substituted with the padyapuja (or foot worship) in which the feet of the deity are covered by a silver covering and then washed.

The entire family was at that time also taken to the store of the Lord's ornaments which was behind seven locked doors. In the light of the earthen lamp, the heaps of diamond-studded gold ornaments were a sight to behold.

I ask Haridas Badve if it is possible to see the vault again. He curtly mentions that had the Badve families been in charge of the temple, he could have managed it, but now these 'government types' were not interested in the old values, and there was a decline in standards. I know exactly what he is referring to but do not comment.

A few families of Brahmins controlled the worship of Vithal over the centuries. The leading group, the Badves, were responsible for taking care of the Lord, with the Utpats taking care of Rukmini. They were entitled to half the revenue received from the devotees, with the other half going to the other sevadars or servants of the Lord who each executed a particular duty.

There were seven types of sevadars. Paricharaks brought the water for the ritual bath of the Lord. The Haridas' sang the arti, the Dingres dressed the Lord and showed him a mirror after the ritual dressing; the Danges stood guard in front of the Lord; the Divates lit and held up the lamps at the time of the rituals and the Benares chanted the mantras. The seventh, the Pujaris, carried out the actual rituals and surprisingly, the Badves, though the chiefs of the lot, were not allowed to touch the idol—this was the sole right of the Pujaris.

A few unscrupulous ones from amongst them extorted money from the pilgrims, and there were even horror stories of some Brahmins murdering pilgrims to steal their ornaments. With financial mismanagement becoming rampant, the government of Maharashtra passed a law in 1973 taking over the administration of the temple, much to the chagrin of the priests who had amassed huge fortunes from the temple. These roles are now given to salaried employees.

I do not counter the mutterings against the government but paying obeisance to the Lord one last time, step out to go to the Rukmini temple, situated just behind the Vithal temple.

Rukmini, also referred to as Rukmai (Rukmini the mother), is worshipped separately from Vithal, and the temple is just behind the temple to Vithal. Her idol is similar in style to the Vithal idol, and she too stands with her hands on her hips. She is angry with Vithal for having no time for her even in Pandharpur and being constantly busy helping his devotees, and hence stands separately.

The smaller temples dotting the periphery also have Satyabhama, Radha, Dattaguru and Kashi Vishveshwara, before whom we bow after a final prayer to Ganesha and exiting from the west gate.

I ask Haridas and my brother-in-law, Vasant, about the controversy surrounding the idol and how it was not the original idol consecrated in the temple many thousand years ago. Haridas vehemently denies that the idol is not the same. He even quotes a couplet from Tukaram saying that this idol was neither crafted nor consecrated since it was the Lord himself who had settled down in Pandharpur.

He mentions that the idol had left the temple only on two occasions—once when carried to Vijayanagara by Krishnadeva Raya and once when the priests shifted it to Tegaon when the forces of Afzal Khan, a general of the Adil Shah dynasty of Bijapur, were running rampant in the area. In each case, he cites historical documents mentioning that the same idol was brought back and reconsecrated in Pandharpur. When I ask him about the absence of the mantra 'Shree Krishanye Namah' on the chest of the deity as mentioned in the various *Vithal Mahatmyas* and the *Skanda Purana*, he is unable to answer suitably. I also ask him about the multiple references in the texts about the idol being that of Krishna in the form of a young boy, as he appeared before Rukmini five hundred years ago in Dindirvana. I mention that the idol currently worshipped seemed to be Krishna at a much later stage of his earthly life and ask them about this, but Haridas is clueless but refuses to budge from his stand that the idol was the same as worshipped over the ages. I tip him for the services rendered, and Vaishali, Vasant, and I head to their home for dinner.

Vasant tells me on the way that in the mid-nineteenth century, some madman threw a stone at the deity and broke the leg of the idol. Not wanting to break the tradition of daily worship, the priests got a new idol sculpted and consecrated it within the night. The idol currently worshipped is the one that was sculpted in a hurry and is hence far from perfect. This fact, he tells me, was something everyone in Pandharpur knew but none would ever admit. It was for them a matter of faith.

For them, this was not an idol; it was Lord Vithal or their own Vithoba—a God who was a member of their own families and with whom, like my grandfather, they felt they had a personal equation.

I turn back to look at the steeple of the temple, close my eyes and ask Vithoba to remember that I had been here and carrying a part of him with me, head back to the car. For days after that, I cannot figure out why I had tears in my eyes all through the evening.

Jai Somnath!

Vikrant Pande

Hundreds of fishing boats lie anchored at the seashore at Veraval as we drive out of the Somnath railway station. The smell of dry fish is overpowering but the quest for the Lord makes us ignore it as we move to the town of Somnath, a few kilometres away. This region, called Prabhas Patan, is a place of worship of both Shiva and Krishna (Vishnu) and thus its uniqueness. And we are here to discover both.

The Somnath temple's magnificent 155-feet-high spire is visible from a distance, with a huge flag fluttering in the sea breeze on a 31-feet-tall post. We are mesmerised at the very sight of the temple. Our driver tells us that the topmost golden kalash weighs approximately 10 tonnes! Another 56 smaller golden kalash on the sloping roof of the temple glint in the evening sun, enticing us to hurry. The facilities to deposit our sandals and phones are conveniently placed and we enter the temple after walking on a long path. The temple brochure tells us that it is built in the Chalukya style of architecture or the 'Kailash Mahameru Prasad' style and reflects the skill of the Sompura Salats, one of Gujarat's master masons and from a branch of the Brahmin community, originally from Somnath.[1] A total of 64 intricately carved pillars support the temple. It faces east and has three entrances. The waves of the Arabian Sea can be heard nearby. Built at the western tip of Gujarat, right at the seashore, we are entering one of the most revered places in India. The temple finds reference in the *Shreemad Bhagwat*, *Skanda Purana*, *Shiva Purana* and the *Rig Veda*.

Chants of Shiva Rudra reverberate as we enter the temple. We are in time for the evening aarti at seven. The sun has just set, leaving the western sky with a golden hue. A group of Brahmins sitting in a corner inside chant together. After a brief silence, when the chanting ends, the drums, cymbals and the trumpets take over and we are enthralled by the captivating atmosphere created all around. It instantly transports us into a different world.

We notice that the Shiva Linga, one of the 12 Jyotirlingas in India, is massive—nearly 4 feet tall. The sanctum sanctorum and the doors are completely gold-plated. But it is the linga which has been the attraction for times immemorial. The popularity of the rituals held at the temple is seen from the list of the poojas available for a devotee to perform. A quick glance at the list takes us by surprise; at the top is the 'Homantak Atirudra' pooja costing a whopping ₹21 lakhs while the 'Mahamrityunjay Jap' and 'Panchopachar' pooja cost a reasonable ₹200! There are in total 39 different poojas one can pay for at the office.

A bath in the sea is supposed to wash off all the sins but the rocky shore which is supposed to be deep as well dissuades us. We notice an interesting structure—the 'Baan Stambh' or the Arrow Pillar situated in the temple premises. An inscription mentions that the arrow points towards the southern direction where one does not encounter any land mass till the South Pole. While the claim may not be fully accurate (there are a few scattered islands on the straight line), it is quite intriguing to find the reference on the pillar which is supposedly hundreds of years old.

The very first thought which comes to our mind when visiting the temple is about Mahmud Ghazni raiding Somnath 17 times. Is it really true? Logistically, it does not seem possible. There are no clear historical references except for a raid in 1026 CE. There is no clear mention of the number of people killed and the gold taken, though various records talk of nearly 50,000 dead and gold equivalent of 20 million dinars having been carted away.

'...Mahmud's destruction of the shrine has been burnt into the collective sub-conscious of the race as an unforgettable national disaster,' wrote Kanhaiyalal Munshi, in his book *Somnath: The Shrine Eternal*, published in 1952.

He further adds, recalling the destruction of the temple many times over thousands of years, 'Its story goes beyond the furthest borders of human ken. Many-a-time has its walls borne the brunt of battle and had been levelled at the hand of the barbarian invader, only to rise from its ashes, like a phoenix, as soon as the enemy had turned its back. The banner of Siva was once again raised aloft above its pinnacles; and the bells, the conch, and the drum once more announced the commencement of worship within.'

'Did you know Ghazni was not here to break the Shiva Linga but a Muslim idol?' asks a guide, Viraj Patel, who introduces himself as we sit on the benches outside the temple and gaze into the sea. Hundreds of boats with small lamps lit on them are bobbing away. They are fishing boats, we are told. It is a pleasant sight but our reverie is broken by his question and we turn to him for explanation. He expects our surprised reaction and refers to a book by Romila Thapar: 'There was an early Arabic goddess called Manat. Somnath could have been a bastardisation of the Arabic "su-manat".' He further elaborates, seeing our baffled faces, 'Manat was one of the goddesses Prophet Muhammad once said could be worshiped, but then retracted, claiming that the assertion was influenced by Satan. These lines came to be known as the "Satanic Verses", and were subsequently deleted from the Quran.

'Romila Thapar also quotes a couple of traditions to say that the image of Manat was "secreted away to Kathiawad for safe keeping in a land where idol worship was considered normal". So, when Mahmud attacked Somnath, he wasn't destroying a Hindu temple but a place that provided sanctuary to a pre-Islamic Arabian goddess!', concludes Viraj.

While it is an interesting theory, we don't find references to this elsewhere. But we are on a quest for stories and folklore, not to challenge them.

We recall the historian Henry Cousens writing of an account by Ferishta. It sounds exaggerated but makes for interesting reading. As per the account, Mahmud Ghazni had struck off the nose of the idol in one blow. He wanted the idol to be broken off and thrown at the threshold of the public mosque and in the court of the palace in Ghazni. A group of Brahmins pleaded by offering crores in gold to stop the marauder from further destroying the temple. While it was a tempting offer, Mahmud continued, as he wanted to be known as a breaker of idols rather than as a buyer. The rejection turned out in his favour. The very next blow revealed that the belly of Somnath was hollow and full of diamonds, rubies and pearls. The invader was pleased as he had got his riches, and also completed the task of breaking the idol.

Our guide continues, 'The original name of Saurashtra was Kushavrata. The place where the Yadavas founded Dwarka was originally called Kushasthali. In ancient times, it was a port of international repute. Prabhas Patan too got its name from the "patan"—the downfall of the Yadava race—which occurred here. Apparently, Krishna's famed Syamantak Mani, the most famous jewel in Hindu mythology, was placed below the Shiva Linga which made the linga float.'

'What is the story of the moon god?' we ask, as we had heard that the temple is named after the moon god.

'In the early days of Creation, the moon god gave light all through the night and every day of the year. But he was biased and loved his wife Rohini more than his other twenty-six wives.'

Viraj interrupts his story to clarify, 'The twenty-seven wives are the twenty-seven constellations in the sky.' We nod, asking him to continue. 'The twenty-six wives complained to their father Daksha Prajapati. Daksha, angry at his son-in-law's behaviour, cursed him that his light would be consumed to extinction. Quite naturally, the people were in distress as they could not spend nights without the cooling light of the moon. The moon god worshipped Shiva for years till he was blessed by the Lord that he would decline for fifteen days and be restored to his luminous self during the remaining fifteen days of the month. The moon god constructed a golden temple for the Lord and that is how the Jyotirlinga came to be known as Somnath, the Lord of the moon god. Thousands of years later, Ravana came to pray here. In his desire to please the Lord, Ravana, instead of offering lotuses to Lord Somnath as was the practice, cut off one head of his after the other and laid it before him. When he was about to chop off his tenth head, the merciful Lord restored his nine heads and gave him the boon which made him the conqueror of the world. As a mark of gratitude, Ravana had a silver temple constructed for the Lord on the spot. After ages, Krishna came to the shrine to pray and built a sandalwood temple. Later, the temple was built in wood, stone and what we see is a modern structure, thanks to K.M. Munshi and Sardar Vallabhbhai Patel,' Viraj concludes with a flourish.

We had read K.M. Munshi's lament in *Somnath: The Shrine Eternal*, when he visited the temple. 'In December 1922 accompanied by a young man, I went to see the shrine before the dawn broke. At that time, I was passing through an emotional crisis and my imagination was aflame with the past glories of Gujarat. We walked for some time on the seashore looking with subdued awe at the majestic ruins of the great temple silhouetted against the starry sky, I remembered our poet Nanalal's verse about Saurashtra where "the sea lashes against its pearly shores". The dawn broke; the aged hoary ruins of this once magnificent temple stood before me. I went into the temple. On the dusty floor of the gudhamandapa, on which once stood the nobles and the mightiest in India, a police sub-inspector had tied a pony! In my first novel in 1915, I had found in Jai Somanatha, the ancient battle cry. But at the plight of this shrine, I broke down.'

Viraj continues his narration. 'It was due to the efforts of Munshi and Sardar Patel that the temple was built to its current glory. Some politicians including Nehru were against President Rajendra Prasad inaugurating it as they felt it would give it a communal angle. But the president prevailed. The president said, at the "prana pratishtha" ceremony (consecration of the idol), "The Somnath temple signifies that the power of reconstruction is greater than the power of destruction."

'Many people then believed that the ruins of the temple should be maintained as an ancient monument, but it was clear to Munshi and Sardar Patel that Somnath was not a monument but it lived in the sentiment of the whole nation and they had pledged to restore its glory. They believed its preservation was not mere historical curiosity but that they owed it to the people of India to give them their revered temple.'

Viraj continues, 'Many rulers earlier have worked for the preservation of the temple after its destruction. Aurangzeb, the fanatic, was the last ruler in whose reign this temple saw the worship of Somnath. In 1706, it was converted into a mosque when he destroyed it. In the same year, the Marathas entered Saurashtra. In 1713, the Marathas conquered Saurashtra-Kathiawar as it was then called. In 1788, Ahalyabai Holkar erected a new shrine away from the much-pillaged temple. In December 1812, the Gaekwad of Baroda acquired control of the shrine from the Nawab of Junagadh.

'The Nawab of Junagadh ran away to Pakistan with his jewels and dogs.' Viraj chuckles here and adds, 'Apparently in the rush, one of his wives and some children were left behind!'

Then continuing, Viraj adds, 'The Jam Sahab of Jamnagar gave the first donation of a lakh of rupees to start the construction. It was completed on 13 May 1965; built at a whopping cost of ₹24,92,000.' When the last detail is mentioned, there is evident pride as if he himself was involved in its construction!

Prabhas Patan is associated with Krishna as it was here that he left his mortal body. We reach a place called Bhalka Teertha, a few kilometres from the Somnath temple. It is a modern structure and the new temple was built only a few years back. The tar on the road is melting in the hot morning sun and the tiles on the temple floor singe our feet as we run to get inside. But Krishna is smiling. The arrow has struck him when he was resting against a peepal tree. Jara, the hunter, assuming it to be a deer, shot his arrow only to realise that he had wounded the Lord himself. He sits guiltily while Krishna smiles. 'The Lord tells Jara that he was Vali in his previous birth and that Krishna, as Rama, had killed him. It was now Jara's turn to redeem the act and that his arrow would become the reason for him to leave the earth,' the priest Dharak tells us, as we gaze at the beautiful idol of Lord Krishna resting against a tree, his right foot placed on his left knee.

The marble statue and the beatific smile brings tears to our eyes. We had a very contrasting experience earlier at Somnath. In the magnetic and surcharged atmosphere of the evening aarti, with the smoke of the sambrani dhoop and blazing oil lamps, the pipes, cymbals and drums sucking away our thoughts, the tears there were of devotion, as we became one with the Lord. Here, at Bhalka Teertha, while Krishna smiles, our tears are of sadness, of personal loss. We feel the pain which he would have gone through. In Somnath, the tears were of spiritual bliss while here, they are an emotional connect with the Lord.

'You see the peepal tree there?' Dharak asks, pointing to an extremely old and knotted trunk emerging from the sanctum sanctorum. 'It comes from the same tree which was here nearly 5,000 years before. This is where Krishna rested,' he says with an assurance which is difficult to challenge.

'It was Gandhari's curse that Krishna would die so,' Dharak elaborates. Seeing our quizzical look, he continues, 'When Gandhari saw her hundred sons dead, she cursed Krishna that he would witness the death of his children and children's children and that he would die alone in a forest hunted down like a beast.'

'Krishna was merely allowing Gandhari's curse to come true,' Dharak continues. 'There is a story of why the arrow hit his toe. Once, as per the wish of Saint Durvasa, Krishna applied payasam or kheer all over his body. As his feet were resting on the ground, he could not apply it there. Durvasa then asked Krishna and Rukmini to pull his chariot. While doing so, he poked Krishna with his stick but that did not rattle Krishna, which impressed the sage. He blessed Krishna, saying no part of the body which had been anointed with the payasam would be the cause of his death. But Krishna had not applied the same to the soles of his feet! And that was to be the cause…' Dharak says, his voice fading away.

'Where did Krishna leave the earth?' we ask Dharak and he guides us to Dehotsarga, a few kilometres away. It is the place where, as Munshi eloquently puts it in his book 'the Lord shuffled off his mortal coil'.

Dehotsarga is just off the Triveni Sangam. We are curious to know about the River Saraswati, but first we reach the place where Krishna 'died'.

'Did he actually die and was he cremated?' we ask the priest there.

'He is the Lord; he cannot be cremated. He simply vanished from here. Which is why we see only his footprints. It was nearly 36 years after the Mahabharata war; some say Krishna was 125 years old,' he explains as he points to a pair of footprints embedded in stone, indicating the place where Krishna left the earth.

At Dehotsarga, K.M. Munshi wrote, 'This spot awakens wonderful memories of Prabhasa Tirtha. I see before me

Balarama, his hands on the shoulders of his wives, enjoying the voluptuous touch of the breezes flowing from the western sea. I see Dharmaraja, the eldest of the Pandavas, coming here on a pilgrimage to the shrine of Somanatha. I see here the stolen glances of Subhadra as she lovingly fastened her gaze on Arjuna walking hand in hand with Sri Krishna on this very bank of the Hiranya. More sombrely I see here the fratricidal war of the Yadavas who, in the plenitude of their power, massacred each other. At Bhalaka Tirtha, I see the Lord Himself sleeping under a tree. I see the hunter's arrow speeding. It enters His feet; He awakens with a shudder: He smiles with superhuman understanding, for His work on earth is done. It is time for me to live forever on His inspiration.

'He has left behind Him unfading memories; of the divine Child on whom everyone doted; of the loyal Friend who never forsook those who came to Him with self-surrender; of the fascinating Love who could love and be loved with undying ardour; of the Rebel who led His people out of bondage; the Yogeshwara who in an age of conflict and rivalries could rise to such a stature that men saw in Him not only their chief, but the embodiment of Indian unity, not merely the World Teacher who stood for Moral Order but God Himself.'

We visit the cave where Balarama disappeared into the earth, as he was the avatar of Shesh Naga, the Lord's serpent.

We ask the priest about the war which Munshi refers to. The Hiranya flows silently and serenely nearby. This is the place where Krishna relieved himself of the burden of being human. The place is frozen in time. It could have been thousands of years back, except for the distant sound of a diesel pump which reminds us of modern times. The birds chirp softly; it is a place to contemplate; to know that He too had to leave the earth and his mortal form.

We sit on a cemented platform around a tree as the priest recounts a story.

'Sage Durvasa used to perform his penance at the Pindara shrine, near Dwaraka. The Yadavas were infamous for their debauched and frenzied behaviour, drunk on youth and power. The Yadavas went berserk under the intoxicating influence of wine, women, wealth, war, gambling and power, and indulged in all kinds of sins. The Yadavas dressed Samb, Krishna and Jambavati's son, as a woman and took him to Durvasa. Without even greeting the sage, they chaffed, laughing aloud, "This woman is Babhru Yadav's wife and is pregnant. Would the child be a girl or a boy?"

'The sage knew a joke was being played on him. Riled by the arrogance and misconduct of the Yadavas, he cursed them saying, "This person will deliver a pestle (moosal), which will result in the annihilation of the entire Yadava race."

'The Yadavas were so petrified that they chose not to tell Krishna about what had happened. As expected, Samb gave birth to a pestle. In order to destroy the evidence, the Yadavas ground it into a fine powder and scattered it into the sea. This grew as the erka grass in Prabhas Kshetra. As the grass grew, it turned into sharper, stronger and ramrod straight blades. Weapons were being readied for the Yadavas! The Yadavas continued to live their lives drunk in power, blissfully unaware of what was happening … so far away from Dwaraka …

'A small piece of that powder which was left uncrushed was swallowed by a fish. It got trapped in a fisherman's net. The fisherman gave the metal piece to a hunter named Jara.

'The hunter Jara fixed the same piece to his arrow …

'Who, but Krishna would know that the same arrow was set to become the reason for the end of his human life …

'Jara aimed at a deer with it …

'A sharp whizz pierced through the air ...

'The toe which had been bathed by Uddhav's tears, stroked by Rukmini's hair, and anointed daily with sandalwood paste was bathed in blood. It seemed as if a spark of fire had entered the body through the toe and left it at lightning speed through the sole.'

The priest had rendered the story in a dramatic fashion and listening to it, we are stunned. We had heard of a story of Krishna's cremation and we could not resist asking the priest about that.

'Yes,' he replied. 'Some people believe that Arjuna cremated Krishna but his heart would not burn. It was then tied to a piece of log and thrown into the ocean. Ages later, it reached the shores of Odisha and it was this log which was used to carve the idols for the Jagannatha temple there.' Another wonderful story!

We silently bowed to the Lord and walked away.

We now moved to the Triveni Sangam, curious to see the Saraswati, Hiranya and Kapila rivers as they merge into the sea.

'As per some sources, the Saraswati emerges from the ground here, while she is underground for most part of her journey from the Himalayas till she reaches Prabhas Kshetra,' a pot-bellied priest sitting there told us.

After popping a wad of tobacco into his mouth, he continued, 'Lord Vishnu once instructed Saraswati to carry "Badwanal" (submarine fire) and dump it in the ocean near Prabhas Kshetra. After taking permission from Lord Brahma, her father, Saraswati flowed towards her destination. As she reached Prabhas Kshetra, four learned sages, who were well-versed in the Vedas arrived there and invoked Saraswati to give them the privilege of separate baths by dividing herself in four different streams. The names of these sages were Hiranya, Vajra, Nyanku and Kapil. When Saraswati reached the ocean, Badwanal was surprised to see the high tides rising in the ocean and wondered if the ocean was scared of him. On Vishnu's advice, Badwanal made himself small, like a needle, but continued to suck the ocean. Finally, Samudra agreed to accept Badwanal. Apparently, the exhalations of Badwanal give us the tides.'

'This is as per the *Skanda Purana*,' he clarifies, seeing our confused faces.

Mythological tales abound here. There can be historical debates but when it comes to myth, local folkore, stories from the Ramayana and Mahabharata, there is little to argue about the authenticity of these tales as that would mean that we are questioning faith itself.

As our car races towards Junagadh, we bow to Lord Shiva once more. We are tempted to visit Dwaraka but that is for another day. At Junagadh, a visit to the Gir forest is an alluring thought to spot the majestic Gir lion. So is the captivating Girnar mountain; a challenge to overcome with its 10,000 steps.

'For those who cannot walk up, there is a modern ropeway now, which takes them to the Amba Mata temple,' our driver tells us, pointing to the pillars of the ropeway silhouetted against the darkening sky.

But our purpose of visit was Somnath and we are content to rest in our hotel, as we recount the stories we have heard the whole day.

Notes

1 The term 'salat' is derived from Shilavat, the old term for a temple architect.

The Sacred and the Profane: Experiencing Khajuraho

Trisha Gupta

The woman climbs the man like a tree. She stands on tiptoe with one leg, her arms clasped around his neck. Her other leg is raised high, bent at the knee. The man holds her calf lightly with one hand, while the other rests gently on the small of her back. It is a position that depends on physical agility, but they seem comfortable in it, elegant and relaxed. What really draws us in, though, is not the sculpted beauty of their entwined limbs, but their sense of languorous surrender—to the moment and each other. She looks up into his face, one hand on the nape of his neck, as if poised to pull him closer. He gazes down at her with gentle eyes, the tilt of his head towards her conveying something intimate and true.

The blissful pair I describe is one of the hundreds of such lovemaking couples carved into the great temples of Khajuraho, their contented sandstone smiles still intact after a thousand years. Of the eighty-odd temples that once existed at the site, only twenty-two remain, most of them covered with sculpted figures and panels, all the way from the jagati—the raised platform at the base—up to the kalasha—the pot-shaped finial at the top. A large number of these carvings are of lovemaking couples, rich with sensual detail. The man's fingers might caress the woman's breast, or close softly around a nipple. Or the woman might arch backwards into her partner's chest, one hand raised behind her head to tug at his anciently stylish man-bun, while the other hovers purposefully at her crotch.

Other depictions are even more explicit. It is common on Khajuraho's walls to see a woman guiding a partner's penis into herself, or riding him while suspended in mid-air, his arms supporting her waist, her feet planted firmly on the wall behind. Further, the erotic encounters on these walls do not limit themselves to penetrative sex, or heterosexual pairings—or even to pairings at all. In many instances, men give each other hand jobs, or one man bends another forward to penetrate him from behind. Other panels have a grandly bejewelled man and a woman at the centre, but they are not alone: female figures on either side lend the couple a hand, or cover their eyes shyly, or a male assistant holds one of their limbs in place, preventing them from tipping over. In ancient Indian artistic convention, the size of a figure relative to another was often an indicator of their social status, so the sakhis and servants are often depicted as much smaller in size.

Alongside these one-on-one encounters are many panels depicting all sorts of group sex, often displaying a puckish sense of humour. In one I remember, a woman hides her face in her hands, looking but not quite looking at her enthusiastically approaching partner. Is her embarrassment explained by the unmissably erect penis which precedes him—or does it spring from the fact that another couple is already at it, right in front of them?

The erotic sculptures are usually described in Hindi as

'kaamuk' (relating to kama, i.e. erotic love and desire, which is one of the four purushaarthas, the four goals of human life in Hindu thought) or 'mithuna' (a lovemaking couple). Their immense variety notwithstanding, these comprise only about 10 per cent of the carvings at Khajuraho. The temple walls—interior and exterior—are covered with all sorts of other sculpted subjects. There are many images of major gods and goddesses like Ganesha, Kubera, Vishnu, Shiva and Parvati; there are family divinities and minor deities; there are real animals and mythical composite animals called vyaalas or shaarduls. There are all sorts of scenes of secular life including grand battles and royal hunts, and a succession of surasundaris—comely young women whose everyday activities have been transformed into artistic tropes: putting kajal in their eyes, rinsing their hair, writing a letter, extracting a thorn from a foot, sometimes just stretching and yawning.

And yet it is the kaamuk and mithuna moortis (figures) that most scholars study, most writers write about and most visitors come to see. For nearly 200 years, since the 'rediscovery' of the temples in 1838, the dusty little village of Khajuraho has become a place synonymous with sex. Even their 'rediscoverer'—a military engineer called Captain T.S. Burt, who took a 44-kilometre detour in a palanquin through what was then dense forest to get there—was 'much delighted at [their] venerable and picturesque appearance', but also shocked by the 'extremely indecent and offensive' carvings on the half-ruined temples.[1]

This mix of rapture and outrage has been the norm, not the exception, in the modern response to Khajuraho.

Our ancestors (if I may be allowed to call the ancient creators and consumers of Khajuraho that for a moment) clearly thought it normal to devote a great deal of time and money, and careful aesthetic attention to the sexual act—or at least to the exploration of it in art. So socially legitimate was this pursuit of kama that it could be carried out on the walls of a public place of worship. As for us moderns? Not just would we be hard put to create anything of the scale or finesse of these temples, we are now confused even about whether to appreciate or condemn them.

***

Khajuraho's tour guides understand this. They are no historians, and they may occasionally misinterpret the temple carvings (sometimes wilfully). But like the makers of a successful formula film, they know their audience.

The Indians who come to Khajuraho are a mixed bunch. The poorer they are, they less likely they are to engage a guide's services—and the more likely they are, too, to do a quick circuit of the Archaeological Survey of India (ASI)-protected complex and make their way to the Matangeshwara Temple just outside, which though dated to around the same time as the rest of the temples, has no carvings and is the only one open for ritual obeisance. For the religious visitor confused by the 'unworshippability' of all the other temples, the guides have a ready response: '*Hindu dharam mein khandit moortiyon ka poojan nahi hota.*' (Broken or damaged idols are not worshipped in the Hindu religion.) The proscription may or may not exist in any one of the thousands of Hindu texts about ritual, but it strategically circumvents any potential debates about whether history and archaeology deserve control of these temples—by keeping the argument on religious terrain.

But for the middle class Indian visitor, how are these temples to be located in the history of modern India? One scholar has suggested that Jawaharlal Nehru took a personal interest in their protection, with his inclusion of Khajuraho in the first Five Year Plan, placing them on the national tourism agenda in the first decade after Independence. This seems plausible, given the late prime minister's deep love of history in general and ancient Indian art in particular: the historian Nayanjot Lahiri has recently written a delightful essay on Nehru's association with the Ajanta and Ellora caves, drawing on his personal letters as well as ASI records of an official visit (on which Edwina Mountbatten also accompanied him).[2] Nehru's interest in Khajuraho, however, remains largely unannotated.

As so often in India, where history leaves a gap, the popular imagination steps in. We need a different version of that old Aristotelian line about nature: in India, culture abhors a vacuum. Nehru didn't serve the purpose, so two other Great Men have found their way into the popular Khajuraho narrative. In this imaginary history, Gandhi wanted Khajuraho demolished and the temples were only saved because Rabindranath Tagore wrote a letter arguing for their preservation.

The story is fiction, but it builds astutely on a few well-known facts. Tagore did, for instance, have frequent differences of opinion with the man to whom he had given the title 'Mahatma', 'Great Soul'.[3] Sometimes these disagreements led to a private correspondence between them. Sometimes Tagore made his disappointment public, such as the grave and prescient warning he issued about the Mahatma encouraging our worst irrationalities when he referred to the Bihar earthquake as a divine punishment for the continued practice of untouchability in society. And Gandhi was, in fact, famously conflicted about sex and sexuality, and a vocal advocate of abstinence for himself and those that wished to walk the path of satyagraha.

The historical conversation between Tagore and Gandhi exemplified the mutually respectful exchange of opposing views that once existed in Indian public life, something that seems impossible to even imagine from within the miasma of personal attacks and whataboutery that masquerades as debate in early twenty-first century India. But the point of popular myth-making is that 'Gandhi' and 'Tagore' are made to go beyond their historical selves, pressed into service to represent two responses to Khajuraho that actually existed in modern Indian society. The fictional Gandhi, featuring here as a sort of appalled elder statesman figure, gives voice to the shock and horror likely frequently felt by the contemporary Indian visitor to the temples. And Tour Guide Fiction isn't half-bad at characterisation—a man who spent much of his life trying to craft a modern Hinduism cleansed of its worst caste prejudices can be imagined to have thought similarly about another aspect of the Hindu past. 'Gandhi' serves as a prism through which we can view Khajuraho's rampant sexuality as an instance of our past excesses—something to be shed in the service of a self-punishing asceticism. Tagore, meanwhile, is cast as the romantic nationalist, the poet of love and lover of beauty, whose model of humanistic education at Santiniketan stood for free-thinking exploration rather than a reining-in of the self.

In their fictional battle over Khajuraho, then, 'Gandhi' and 'Tagore' step in to represent the conflictedness of the modern Indian response to a site whose splendidly executed carvings are equally a measure of past artistic greatness, and incontrovertible proof of an unabashedly sexual heritage.

Would modern India rather erase her sexual history, or proudly lay claim to it?

***

Indian tourists, of course, were not the first priority when the Indian government first decided to develop Khajuraho as a heritage destination in the 1950s. Protected by the ASI, the twenty-two surviving temples at Khajuraho continue to be identified by the monikers given them in the mid-nineteenth century by Alexander Cunningham, first director-general of the ASI: the Western Group, the Eastern Group and the Southern Group. The Eastern and Southern groups are not collectively landscaped or ticketed, though many of the individual temples have received the standard ASI treatment: a plaque inscribed with architectural details, a small lawn surrounding the structure, a gated boundary wall around the lawn, and a single, usually taciturn, security guard at the gate. Meanwhile, the Western Group—a ticketed rectangular complex including the Lakshmana, Kandariya Mahadev and Devi Jagadambi temples, which was declared a UNESCO world heritage site in 1986—ranks consistently among the Indian monuments most visited by foreigners. The ASI figures from ticket sales in 2018 show that it had 80,000 foreign visitors that year, in tenth place (the Taj Mahal tops the list, with 7,90,000 foreigners having bought tickets to see it that year).

In the fiscal year 2020, only about 42,000 foreigners visited the site, a stark drop that probably has to do with the lockdowns and travel restrictions put in place from March 2020. But even before the Covid-19 pandemic made international travel impossible, the proportion of foreign tourists at Khajuraho has been slowly dropping—as have their absolute numbers. Between 2006 and 2015, the annual count of foreign tourists in Khajuraho declined from 73,843 to 65,034. The number of Indian visitors, meanwhile, is growing. In 2006, only 1,64,000 Indians visited these temples. By 2015, that number had risen to 2,79,000. For the year 2018, the ASI reported that foreigners visiting the Western Group of temples numbered less than 61,000, while the number of Indian visitors had risen to 3,61,594—that's over 3 lakh more Indians than foreigners.

While there are less foreign tourists coming, a larger proportion of those who arrive are likely to spend the extra amount needed for guides. More studies are needed to make the argument conclusively, but the exponential rise in Indian tourists at the site has probably begun to affect how Khajuraho is described and understood by its guides. Indian visitors—most of whom recognise the major Hindu gods and goddesses and have certain ideas about temples—are an audience very different from the average Western tourist who could possibly be fobbed off with historically dubious references to 'the Kama Sutra temples'.

But what really makes the Khajuraho tour guide's task difficult is the delicacy with which Indian visitors need to be drawn into the sexual aspects of the temples. For far too many Indians, sex is either something muffled and awkward that you do hurriedly in the dark and hide all evidence of—or a much-fetishised item on an aspirational list of achievements that you need to pretend you have lots of. Swinging between the guilty secret and the fake boast, we know little and judge a lot.

And yet it is sex that brings most Indians to Khajuraho.

The biggest category of Indian visitors, my guide tells

me, are young married couples. For at least twenty years, the temples have also made this landlocked Madhya Pradesh outpost a favoured holiday destination for those in the throes of romance. If the just-marrieds are enticed by the attractive honeymoon packages, there's a carrot for the others, too—or at least the absence of the usual stick. An internet search for budget hotels in Khajuraho throws up a 'Hotel Rule' still rare enough in India to read as both assurance and advertisement: 'Unmarried Couples Allowed'.

The other frequently seen category of Indian tourists is the all-male group of young students, wandering through the temples with their arms around each other, pointing and laughing. A recent study by a Lucknow-based anthropologist suggests that 29 per cent of tourists visit the temples for the explicit carvings—'not interested in understanding the history and architecture, they only come to look'.[4] Indians, she claims, make up the bulk of that number.

***

So, most Indians are there for the sexy sculptures, but don't want to be treated as if they are. That double standard is the unspoken basis of the tour guide narrative. It shapes both the form and content of the genre, beginning with the telling of Khajuraho's ancient past. Thus, if the scholarly version of Khajuraho's history foregrounds conquest, religion and architecture, the tour guide version manages to foreground sex. Or more accurately, a mythical sexual encounter.

Let me explain. If you read an academic art historian like Devangana Desai, the history of Khajuraho begins when the Chandella prince Yashovarman conquers the nearby hill fortress of Kalinjar, throws off the yoke of his Pratihara overlords, takes an iconic Vishnu statue from the Pratihara king Devapala, and commissions the first sandstone temple (the Lakshmana Temple, consecrated in 954 CE as the abode of Vaikuntha, Vishnu, as the enemy of demons)—as well as a huge water tank (likely today's Shivsagar).

The Tour Guide version prefers to take things further back—*and* make them steamier. One night in Banaras, the story goes, a pretty young woman called Hemavati (who was the daughter of a priest called Hemraj), found herself burning up with lust. To cool off, she decided to take a midnight swim. But the vision of Hemavati in the water was so tempting that Chandra Dev, the moon, decided to descend to earth in human form to make love to her. The product of this 'madhur milan' was Chandravarman, first of the Chandellas.

'Belief or disbelief is up to you,' my guide said, perhaps observing my sceptical expression. '*Main khud* science student *raha hoon*' (I was a science student myself), he added generously, hinting that we might be in agreement. The myth doesn't figure in the Chandellas' own historical records. It appears to be a bardic addition made in later medieval texts like the *Mahoba-Khanda*, *Varna Ratnakara*, *Prithviraj Raso* and *Kumarapala-charita*, claiming a genealogy that's half-divine, half-mortal (unsurprisingly for Indian dynastic claims, the mortal half is Brahmin). Versions of the tale do exist on the internet, but they do not mention Hemavati being (as my guide put it) 'kaam se vyaakul' (desperate with desire). Khajuraho's guides, however, appear to take special pleasure in that salacious detail. It sets the perfect tone: myth + sex, dressed up as dynastic history.

Of course, a careful line needs to be drawn between the

juicy and the inappropriate—especially with female visitors. My guide spent several initial minutes telling me that he had been showing people round the temples for over fifteen years, that he had recently accompanied a single woman client (with a car and driver) on a five-day trip around the region, and that I could speak to her if I so wished. In other words, that his character was vouched for.

Having thus insured himself, he proceeded to draw attention to the sexy carvings by delicately offering to *not* discuss them: 'Madam, can I show you the erotic sculptures, or otherwise I will leave it…?' Having reassured me, he now wanted reassurance. Only once I made clear that I wasn't going to take offence did he begin to point out all sorts of sexual positions and practices, often observed in the breach.

One young woman, he said, was being punished for bestiality by the king. A set of depictions of oral sex elicited a practiced spiel: '*Soch ke dekhiye: jo videshon mein aaj kar rahein hain, apne poorvaj hazaar saal pehle kar ke chhod chukey!*' (Think about it: what people do now in foreign countries, our ancestors finished with a thousand years ago!) The 'kar ke chhod chukey' (finished with it) is a masterful touch. In one fell swoop, it suggests that while Indian civilisation was, in sex as in all things, far in advance of the rest of the world, we were done and dusted with it a thousand years ago—so there was no need to think about its occurrence in present-day sanskaari India!

A little later, having asked me to spot the difference between two near-identical surasundaris, he was thrilled when I said one might conceivably look happier than the other. '*Shayad nahi, aisa hi hai! Hum log* vulgarity *mein nahin jaate* madam, *lekin yeh hai* satisfied *aur yeh* unsatisfied,' he gestured first to the smiling statue and then the other.

Then, looking rather satisfied himself, he turned back to me for the punchline. '*Yeh hai* art!'

***

Along with the Konarak Temple in Odisha and Vatsyayana's *Kama Sutra*, Khajuraho is repeatedly invoked as authentic and indisputable proof of our sexually expressive past. Whenever liberals bemoan what the anthropologist William Mazzarella has humorously called the Great Indian Repression (a little-understood historical shift often incorrectly attributed to the coming of Islam and then Christianity),[5] the mention of Khajuraho is de rigueur,[6] whether in anti-censorship legal arguments—or these days, snarky internet comebacks.

In late 2020, to offer just one recent instance, BJP politicians in Madhya Pradesh filed objections to a scene in Mira Nair's Netflix adaptation of Vikram Seth's *A Suitable Boy* where the (Hindu) heroine Lata is seen kissing her (Muslim) college mate Kabir. The Hindu-Muslim love affair was thrown in as clickbait, but the question the BJP MP asked on social media was why the kiss had to be shot in the 'praangan' (outer courtyard) of a temple. In response, a meme started to do the rounds of Twitter. It contained a screenshot of the controversial lip-lock, captioned 'Boycott Netflix for kissing scene in temple'—and just below it, one of the famous mithuna images from the Viswanatha Temple at Khajuraho, where the couple is locking more than just lips, with a caption that read simply, 'The temple'.

Khajuraho's very mention can shut down narrow Hindutva claims about the nature of Hinduism. But it deserves to be more than a liberal talisman, a name we pronounce to ward off the evil Sanatani eye. Khajuraho might seem to serve as the definitive liberal answer to many things, but surely our first task is to let it spark questions!

The questions that arise for the visitor to Khajuraho are threefold. One, how can such frank depictions of sex be art? Two, even if we grant its artistic quality, how can it be religious? And three, closing the loop: how can religion be so sexual?

The search for answers requires one to walk at least a little way along several different paths: aesthetic, philosophical, historical, sociological—and sexual. And as you start walking, the different paths turn out to be rather more intertwined than you imagined.

Perhaps the first task at hand is the simplest—or the most difficult: to stop seeing all sex as porn. Would it help, one wonders, to see these rambunctious, sensual, unabashed embraces through ancient eyes? How did the sculptors of Khajuraho see it? How did the people who once worshipped Shiva or Vishnu in these temples see the multiplicity of sexual acts all around them? We know less than we might want to about how the erotic carvings were viewed when the temples were active places of worship, but it might help to piggyback on historians of Indian art and religion. Namit Arora, in a chapter on Khajuraho in his book *Indians: A Brief History of a Civilisation* (2021), has summarised a lot of the relevant historical scholarship. He cites Devangana Desai, who calls the religion of Khajuraho 'a synthesis of two religious orders, Tantric and Puranic, resulting in a Misra (mixed or composite) religion' which included 'Vedic mantras and caste-order along with the Tantric mode of worship'.[7]

The word 'tantra' literally means 'woven together', in

Sanskrit, and might be most simply understood as a weaving together of the physical with the philosophical, the sexual with the spiritual, the body with the mind. Unlike Brahminical Hinduism, and also unlike Buddhism and Jainism, Tantrism does not see the body or its desires as an impediment to spiritual enlightenment. In fact, writes Robert L. Brown in *The Roots of Tantra*, the Tantric practitioner was expected to achieve both enlightenment and worldly success, and the way to reach these dual goals was by 'connecting themselves to a power that flows through the world, including their own bodies, a power usually visualised as female'.[8] '[T]he ultimate tool in Tantra,' writes Brown, 'is the human body… both the anatomical body of arms, hands, tongue, heart, genitals, and mind, and the yogic anatomy of cakras and nadis.'[9] Tantric beliefs and practices never became an organised religion. But they did acquire great popularity in North India in the mid-first millennium CE, attracted many wealthy and royal followers, and 'in *mild* forms, spanning goddess worship and meditative practices … broadly pervaded all Hindu, Buddhist and Jain sects'.

'[A]ssociated with fertility cults, amorous motifs and symbols, magic and alchemy, sexo-yogic practices, and a higher status for women,' writes Arora, Tantra furnished the Chandella elites with a worldview in which sex and religion, far from being divergent pursuits, were seen as deeply connected. So putting sex on temple walls had absolute intellectual-philosophical sanction. Moreover, Devangana Desai, in a brilliantly erudite bit of historical detective work, establishes convincingly that the sexual sculptures were also complicated puns in both literary and architectural terms. 'Slesha' or double meaning was a high form of artistic achievement at the time, and Khajuraho's sculptors were masters of the double entendre.[10]

But it would be ridiculous to think that either the creators or consumers of sexual images were only being high-minded artists making philosophical puns. We are still talking about sex, after all—and the pleasure that human beings derive from looking at depictions of it is only second to the pleasure they derive from having it. So a lot of the explicit sex pictured at Khajuraho would have also served exactly the same purpose as it does now: to titillate, entertain, stimulate the masses. Sex on the walls, in other words, meant different things to different people—and that was all right.

Perhaps the difference was that the Indian mind had not then separated everything from everything else. Perhaps it wasn't yet a society in which a man showing someone around the temples can admiringly proclaim the huge girth of the Shiva Linga in the Matangeshwara Mandir—but feels he has to drop his voice to a whisper to say the word 'kaamuk'.[11] Perhaps we sensed more easily then that the kaamuk which gives us individual pleasure is the same thing being collectively celebrated in an ancient fertility ritual, or in the mythical weddings of the gods.

Ye old Captain Burt, while claiming credit for finding these 'lost' temples, had noted that thousands of yogis seemed to find their way to them each year on Shivaratri.[12] It is deeply reassuring that the night of Shiva and Parvati's wedding remains Khajuraho's biggest festival even in the twenty-first century.[13] A huge annual mela is held on the occasion, which runs for several days, and some 25,000-odd people walk in a procession to assemble at the Matangeshwara Temple, where the Shiva Linga is dressed in a bridegroom's clothes.

'*Bakayada baaraat aati hai* (it's a proper wedding procession)', said my guide expansively. I realised just how proper when he proceeded to tell me that the ASI were 'the girl's side' and the nagar panchayat officials were 'the boy's side'.

From a distance, Khajuraho may look like a blip in our history, its evidence of our capacity for sexual jouissance a lonely little peak in the dry, flat desert of the subcontinent's present-day reality. But it still casts a long shadow. And for many Indians, it is a welcome bit of shade—one in which we might pause to re-experience our relationship to the sexual. Because what Khajuraho still makes you see, even in its muddled modern avatar, is that sex can be embodied and transcendent, profane and sacred, at the same time. In fact, it often is.

Notes

1 T.S. Burt in the *Journal of the Asiatic Society*, 1838, cited in Shobhita Punja, *Khajuraho: The First Thousand Years*, Penguin, 2010.

2 Nayanjot Lahiri, *Archaeology and the Public Purpose: Writings on and by M.N. Deshpande*, Oxford University Press, 2021.

3 Gandhi, in turn, referred to Tagore as 'the Great Sentinel'. 'I regard the Poet,' he said, 'as a sentinel warning us against the approach of enemies called Bigotry, Lethargy, Intolerance, Ignorance, Inertia and other members of that brood.' Cited in *Rabindranath Tagore: An Anthology*, ed. Krishna Dutta and Andrew Robinson, St. Martin's Griffin, 1998.

4 'Khajuraho: Tourism and Its Impact', Shuchi Srivastava, http://www.heritageuniversityofkerala.com/JournalPDF/Volume6/61.pdf.

5 In fact, this rejigging of the Indian mind has to do with transitions within Hinduism, from a time when Tantra and

sexo-yogic practices shared the stage with more ascetic strains, to an era where popular religion came to be dominated by Bhakti: devotional surrender to a personal god. The Bhakti saints were anti-caste and anti-ritual, but the devotional love they spoke of was all about the soul, transcending the body (rather than trying to work through it). Between Bhakti and the return of orthodox Brahminism, it is the renunciatory, often masculine, strain of Hindu thought that has come to hold sway in North India over the last four or five centuries. (This is, of course, a very broad claim, to which there are many exceptions—for instance, any pockets where the worship of the mother goddess is still strong.)

6 William Mazzarella, *Censorium: Cinema and the Open Edge of Mass Publicity*, Orient Blackswan, 2013.

7 Devangana Desai, *The Religious Imagery of Khajuraho* (1996), cited in Arora, 2021.

8 Robert L. Brown, Introduction to Katherine Harper and Robert L. Brown, ed. *The Roots of Tantra*, 2002.

9 Ibid.

10 Devangana Desai, 'Puns and Enigmatic Language in Sculpture', in *The Religious Imagery of Khajuraho* (1996).

11 Although I should note here that the Shiva Linga is a symbol not of unrestrained sexuality, but its opposite—sexuality in a contained state. 'Shiva's great powers are directly associated with his sexual abstinence,' writes the anthropologist Lawrence A. Babb in *The Divine Hierarchy: Popular Hinduism in Central India* (1975), going on to cite the Sanskrit scholar Wendy O'Flaherty, who wrote in 1969: 'Siva is the natural enemy of Kama... because he is the epitome of chastity, the eternal brahmacarin, his seed drawn up...' But as Babb also points out, the fact that worshipping the Shiva Linga involves pouring water over it to 'cool' it suggests that the linga is ritually 'hot'. Shiva's 'heat-power'

thus derives not from a lack of arousal, but from restraint in the context of arousal.

12 Burt, cited in Punja, 2010. Burt also seems to suggest that unlike the other temples, which had fallen into disuse and partial ruin, the Matangeshwara Temple retained its sacred aura as a place of worship: '...while I was at this last temple, the natives objected to my going inside without taking off my boots. There was a huge lingam inside this one, eight feet in height and four feet in diameter.'

13 Shiva is a multi-layered God. Yes, he is the great yogi, but he is powerfully sexual. In the rite of Gaura, along with his wife, the Goddess Parvati, he is also associated with ritual possession. His wedding procession on Shivaratri was accompanied by drunken demons, and of course Shiva is believed to be fond of bhang, which is widely consumed on Shivaratri—and makes for frenzy rather than control. (Babb, 1975)

Shivratri at Killa Katas

Haroon Khalid

Raindrops touch the surface of the turquoise pond resulting in tiny ripples. Small fish gather around underwater plants. A young child puts his finger into the water. The fish scatter. His friend is amused by the trick. 'Stay away from the water,' shouts Shakeel, as he notices the children playing at the steps of the pond from afar. Although they are standing away from the deep side of the water, he feels that he still needs to keep a vigilant eye on them. These are Hindu children who have come from Gujranwala and Shakeel is not too fond of them. There are a few Hindu adults nearby, busy preparing for the night, for which about two thousand pilgrims would pour in from different parts of the country, ready to celebrate Shivratri.

Wearing a brown shalwar kameez with a thick shawl wrapped around his body, Shakeel is heading towards the haveli of Hari Singh Nalwa, a general in the army of Maharaja Ranjit Singh (1780-1839), the erstwhile ruler of Punjab. The haveli is his favourite part of the complex. It's a giant structure, the tallest here, standing like a cube with a small dome at the top. The artwork has been recently renovated with depictions of Hindu deities on the walls, including that of Ganesh, an obese Hindu god who has the head of an elephant. Pictures of Krishna, standing cross-legged and playing the flute while he flirts with the maidens, have been painted intricately.

In the past five years, ever since he was employed here, Shakeel has perfected sentences in English, which he uses eloquently to impress his audience. 'Ganesh was the son of the Hindu God, Shiva. Once Shiva went. Shiva's wife had a son while he was gone. Once she take a bath and ask Ganesh to stand at the gate, to guard. When Shiva come, Ganesh stop him. Angry, the Shiva cut his head off. When his mother saw, she cried terribly and Shiva realised that he is his son. He then take a head of a elephant and put it on Ganesh.' His English is not yet perfect, but he is confident of what he says. Experience has also taught him how to slip in personal information about himself, subtly mentioning his hardships and his will to study more, yet not being able to, because of the lack of resources. This usually works in his favour and he ends up with a good tip by the time he finishes off the tour. He always starts his story with the pond.

The turquoise pond changes its colour at the shallower ends. It is round. A rock placed underneath the pond separates a small section of it from the larger body of water. This holds clear water, only three feet deep. Plants growing at the base can be seen from the surface. Ancient buildings stand at the edge of the deeper end, covering it from that side. Balconies and alleys open up towards the water. The structure, which is light brown in colour, shows signs of weathering, its perfect reflection visible in the water. The pond is clearly the lifeline of this complex. Numerous myths have developed around it. 'No one knows how deep it is,' Shakeel explains to the tourists.

'Several attempts have been made to check the length, but no one ever touch the base. There are poisonous lizards and snakes living inside,' he tells everyone. These are some of the ancient stories that have been passed on for generations. 'If you look at the pond from the top, you will see that it is in the shape of an eye. The Hindus believe that when Shiva's (the Hindu deity of destruction) wife Sati dead, he shed a tear, which fall at this place and this pond was created. Another tear fall in Ajmer Sharif, India, where there is another ancient pond, like this one.'

Shakeel, a twenty-five-year-old graduate, lives in Kalar Kahar, a few kilometres away from here. The Archaeology Department appointed him and a few other people as guides for the location when it was renovated. He mentions that he wants to do his master's in archaeology from Punjab University, Lahore. 'The truth is that this is an ancient area. Several million years ago, this place was under the sea. When it emerged, this pond was formed,' he says. He picks up a piece of rock from the ground and asks the tourists to look at it carefully. There is a fossil of a leaf on it. 'There are hundreds of such rocks here, all from that time when this area was underwater.' Later he takes the tourists into a cave, across the road from the complex. It has a small entrance. Cone-shaped structures hang from the roof. These are mineral deposits called stalactites. Shakeel picks up another piece of rock from here, which has a fauna fossil, and hands it over to one of the female photographers in the group. 'This is my gift to you,' he says with a smile.

Next to the haveli he points out a Buddhist stupa that has been partially excavated. 'This is from the third century BCE, from the time of Taxila (an ancient city, near Islamabad, with ruins dating back to the sixth century BCE),' says Shakeel. This is a huge round structure with untrimmed grass growing on it. This must have been a plinth of the stupa. More than half of the structure is still underground. Climbing a few steps, Shakeel leads the tourists to the ancient Hindu temples. According to him, the three tall cone-shaped structures are from the time of the Mahabharata. 'When the Pandavas were exiled from their kingdom, they came and settled here and constructed these temples at that time,' he tells the curious crowd around him. His story is confirmed by a blue board put up by the authorities here, noting the date of Mahabharata to be around 1500 BCE.

Across the road, Shakeel takes his group to the top of a mound that overlooks the temple complex. On the other side one can see a vast plain, interspersed with a few houses and restaurants. Taking the tourists to the edge, he points to an ancient staircase leading up to the mound. 'These were used to get to the university,' he says pointing to a newly constructed single storey rectangular structure. 'This was the site of a world famous ancient Hindu university. Al-Beruni, a Muslim scholar from the eleventh century, studied Hindu religion at this university. Here he also calculated the radius of world, the first time anyone ever did. Muslim scholars were famous world over at that time,' says Shakeel, hurrying to finish off the tour in his professional tour guide manner.

As the night descends, the sky clears off and it stops raining for a little while. The full moon illuminates the area otherwise engulfed in darkness. The wind is chilly. Millions of stars shine in the backdrop of the darkness, adding richness to the sky. A lone sound of someone playing the flute floats in from a distance, breaking the utter silence. Al-Beruni probably sat here for countless nights under this sky, gaping at the stars, astonished at their beauty. He would have made friends with them as he attended to their light out here, all alone. He used these stars to calculate the radius of the world. He was the very first one in the world to do so. Noticing that his group is lost in the beauty of the stars, Shakeel interrupts by announcing that he is leaving. Surprised, the female photographer takes out a thousand rupee note from her bag and gives it to him. 'No, please! There is no need for this,' he objects. 'I insist,' she says. Shrugging his shoulders he takes the note and puts it in his pocket, leaving the tourists under the open sky.

***

Al-Beruni came to India during the first half of the eleventh century, after the Muslim invader Shah Mahmood Ghaznvi attacked Punjab. Al-Beruni arrived at this temple, which was known as a seat of learning at that time. He spent several years here, learning and reading about the language, religion and culture of the Hindus. Experts say that these temples were constructed between the seventh and tenth century CE, when this area was under the influence of the Kashmiri kingdom. Al-Beruni compiled his observations in a book called *Al-Hind*, which is considered to be one of the best anthropological works of all time. It is the first study which introduced the Indian people and their religion to the western world. In his book, he claims that the Hindus are believers of one God, like the Muslims, and are *Ahl-e-Kitab* or the 'Followers of the Book', a term used in the Muslim holy book, the Quran, to refer to the Christians and the Jews. By referring to the Hindus as the followers of the book, Al-Beruni raises their status in the eyes of the Muslim readers and urges them to not view them as 'lowly pagans' but rather followers of the same God that they worship. The title also permits the Muslims to have food with the Hindus and intermarry. However, in contemporary Pakistan, where nationalism is premised upon hatred for Hindus, such a claim would not only be shunned but also taken offence to.

This complex—with a natural pond, fossils dating back to millions of years, ancient caves, an unexcavated Buddhist stupa, Hindu temples said to be thousands of years old, and a university which attracted scholars from other parts of the world—is known as Katas Raj or Killa Katas. Situated near the small town of Kalar Kahar, this is a complex of immense historical significance. The presence of ancient structures here points towards the fact that this has been a holy site for thousands of years. In his pursuit of spiritual enlightenment, the founder of the Sikh religion, Guru Nanak (1469-1539), also came here, as it was a popular destination for ascetics at that time.

There are several small temples built around the pond, dedicated to different Hindu deities. Today, an iron fence protects the complex from its surroundings and only one entrance leads into it. However, there are other ways of entering the temple, especially if one is adamant, and one such way is by climbing the mound. Across the road, next to the mound where the university was situated, there is a newly constructed single storey building. This was constructed a few years ago and now acts as the Archaeology Department office. Major renovation work of the temple was undertaken by the department in 2005.

After the pond was cleaned and the buildings were painted and restored, blue boards were raised around the area, highlighting the significance of particular spots in the area.

Katas Raj was a popular religious site for the Hindus before the Partition. Thousands of pilgrims used to descend here from faraway places on the occasion of Shivratri, a Hindu festival dedicated to the worship of Lord Shiva. This temple was abandoned as a result of the Partition, resulting in the buildings falling into disrepair and the pond being polluted. Over the years, a few cement factories opened in the surrounding area and started sucking the water out from here. There was no one to guard the shrine from the people of the neighbouring villages and cities, who would often visit and leave their marks on the temple walls. Several phone numbers and names are still engraved on them, a testimony of those years of neglect. A few Hindus would visit occasionally, pretending to be tourists exploring the ruins. However, given their small number, they were not able to exert enough pressure to rectify the damage done to their holy shrine.

Prem Gupta, a forty-year-old Hindu activist from Lahore, visited Katas Raj for the first time in 2003. 'There were boys jumping from the windows and alleys of temples into this sacred pond. They would leave juice boxes and chips wrappers in the water,' he recalls. For the Hindus, this pond believed to be created from the tear of Lord Shiva, is holy. They believe that a dip in the pond will cleanse them of their sins.

Things changed for the shrine in 2005, when the veteran Indian politician L.K. Advani came here and expressed displeasure at the neglect of the authorities. In response, the Government of Pakistan started renovation work. In the subsequent year, the government invited Indian pilgrims to visit the shrine on the occasion of Shivratri. About three hundred pilgrims came, which became national news. As a result, the shrine became popular. Several local tourists started coming here. Local Hindus, who did not know about it earlier, also started to visit. The Indian pilgrims would stay here for three days, during which the government would ensure security and shelter for them. They would reside at the building, at the site of the ancient university where they would be given free food. The entire area would be cordoned off while the Indians visited and no one would be allowed to come into the complex. This continued until 2008. But after the Mumbai attacks in which the city was held hostage between 26–29 November 2008 and resulted in the death of several locals and foreigners, allegedly at the hands of Pakistani terrorists, the relationship between India and Pakistan which had been warming up, nosedived. Pilgrims didn't come to Katas for Shivratri in 2009.

For the local Hindus, this proved to be an opportunity. In 2010, a few Hindu organisations met and decided that they would celebrate the festival of Shivratri here that year. 'We wrote to the Archaeology Department, Evacuee Trust Property Board (ETPB, an organisation that looks after the property of non-Muslim shrines. It is also referred to as Hindu Awqaf or Wakf), police, Ministry of Minorities, and so forth, asking for permission to celebrate the festival of Shivratri at Katas Raj,' says Prem Gupta, who is the head of the Hindu Sudhar Sabha, one of the organisations involved. The Hindus did not receive any response. Gupta, who also works at a local NGO and often travels to remote corners of the country, is familiar with the red tape of the bureaucracy. Along with other organisations, they decided to go ahead with the celebration. About two thousand Hindus came to Katas from various cities of Pakistan unannounced, including Lahore, Rahim Yar Khan, Peshawar and Nowshera, and celebrated Shivratri. Encouraged by the success, the Hindus decided to organise the celebration again in 2011.

***

While Shakeel showed the visitors around Katas, Gupta stood at the gate of the complex, busy with the preparations. He has put up a banner at the entrance which reads, 'Welcome Yatrees (pilgrims)' in English, a language that the majority of his guests are unfamiliar with. There is a large picture of Lord Shiva on it. A snake is coiled around his neck. A third eye, which he can use to destroy the world, is visible on his forehead. The moon is in his hair and one hand is lifted up to bless the devotees. A few other workers are putting up a canopy inside the complex, where the pilgrims are expected to stay. Gupta knows that there is not enough space for everyone out here. Besides, it is too cold to sleep in the open.

The date is 2 March 2011. It has been raining all day, which has caused the temperature to drop by several degrees. A few Hindu families have already arrived and are helping Gupta with the preparations. The children are playing next to the pond. Some women are visiting the shrines while others have gone to the restaurant down the road. A few police officials stand at the gate with Gupta. The local guides have informed the police that Hindus are planning to celebrate the event here, for which they do not have official permission. These are only five officials, who watch closely as Gupta sets up the banner and the tent. They have been placed here to look after the security of the thousands of pilgrims who will descend here. The number of officials deployed is an indication of the scant importance that Hindu pilgrims are accorded.

A group of college girls arrive accompanied by a professor. They have come from the National College of Arts (NCA, established in Lahore in 1857; it is considered to be the most prestigious art college in the country). They are stopped at the gate by the police officials. 'Muslims are not allowed inside today,' says one of them to the professor. Gupta standing nearby gives him a smile and gets back to instructing the workers. The professor stays for a little while, looking at the ongoing preparations. Then without resistance he takes his students to the caves, after which they will return to Lahore. Another group of boys try to enter the complex and are also stopped by police officials. 'Let them go,' says Gupta, as he walks away talking over the phone. These are Hindu boys. Gupta's eighteen-year-old son, Vinod, hands the boys a tag. It reads 'Maha Shivratri' with a picture of Lord Shiva, similar to the banner placed at the entrance. 'Let in anyone carrying this identification pass,' Gupta instructs the police officers.

A tall sturdy man with hazel eyes, Prem Gupta is based in Lahore, where he lives with his family near the famous Muslim shrine, Bibi Pak Daman. He visits the shrine often, which is associated with the Shia sect of Islam, but is also visited by Sunni Muslims, all part of the religious syncretism that was once part of this land but is now vanishing. He resides there with his father, mother, wife, children, brothers, nephew, nieces and uncles. In a neighbourhood dominated by Muslims, theirs are the only Hindu houses. Unlike the majority of the Hindus, living in Lahore, they have refused to take up dual names. His father still calls himself Shami Lal. His eldest son, Vinod, is a second year student at the Forman Christian College, Lahore, one of the oldest colleges set up by Christian missionaries, under the 5 per cent reserved seats for minorities. His entire family has come for the festival.

'There is some terrible news,' Gupta comes back from his phone call. 'Shahbaz Bhatti has been murdered this morning in Islamabad, outside his residence. I have just been told,' he says. Bhatti, a Roman Catholic, was the federal minister for minorities when he was assassinated. A vocal critic of oppression against minorities, Bhatti recently had focused on the blasphemy laws, which are used to target minorities in Pakistan. A couple of months ago, the Governor of Punjab, Salman Taseer was gunned down by his bodyguard in Islamabad for criticising the law. It was being assumed that Bhatti had also been killed for his views. 'Everyone is scared,' Gupta adds. 'They were on the way when the news came. What is happening in this country?' Gupta does not stop the preparations; he heads to the restaurant to recover from the trauma.

***

Down the road, there is a small building, the only restaurant in the area. A few pilgrims, who have arrived, are gathering here. The waiters are busy serving tea and garam roti. The owner, sitting behind his table, is watching the news covering the assassination of the minister earlier in the day. The restaurant is full. Just a few years ago, this place would have refused to serve these people, ironically following a tradition that upper caste Hindus used to practise against Muslims in the pre-Partition days. But now things have changed and untouchability, at least here, has receded to the background. The restaurant has the only washroom the pilgrims can use. It would close at eleven in the night, after which the pilgrims would once again have to camp out in the open. Tindas (round gourd) are available for dinner, but none of the pilgrims are having it. They are saving themselves for the langar in the night.

Hindu pilgrims from Peshawar have arrived in two large buses. This group is headed by forty-two-year-old Haroon Sarab Diyal. President of the All Pakistan Hindu Rights Movement (another organisation responsible for arranging this pilgrimage), Diyal is one of the most famous Hindu activists in the country. His statements regarding minority issues often appear in the national newspapers. There are about a hundred people with him: women, children, men and the elderly.

'There are more buses on the way,' he tells Gupta, upon arrival. These are two from Nowshera (Khyber Pakhtunkhwa). Gupta tells him that the buses from Rahim Yaar Khan and Bahawalpur are also on their way. Contrary to the stereotype of being a religiously oppressive area, since the Partition, the province of Khyber Pakhtunkhwa (KPK) has been home to a large proportion of religious minorities who have lived there rather peacefully. These are primarily Hindus, who form the largest minority. Thousands of them are part of the mainstream society, visible often in the economic and political fabric, which is hardly the case in Punjab, which is much more monolithic. Hindu festivals are celebrated with much pomp in these areas; more so than in Lahore. 'If you want to see the lights of Diwali, go to Peshawar. You will find nothing in Lahore,' Gupta often jokes. The primary reason for that is that unlike Punjab, the riots were less intense due to the influence of the Indian National Congress there. A lot of Hindus and Sikhs continued living in their ancestral lands even after the creation of Pakistan.

Diyal is not happy with the arrangements at the temple. There is no electricity and it is dark by now. A tubelight in the courtyard of the Archaeology Department is the only light in the surroundings. The tents have been set up, but hardly anyone is resting here. A few old men, too tired to stand in the rain, have laid out their bedding on the ground and are lying down inside the complex. Diyal has brought a generator with him, fearing the worst. He asks a few boys to set it up. They plan to light a bulb at the temple on their own.

'The authorities have not paid the bill of this temple for the past three months. Electricity has been cut off therefore,' says an angry Diyal. There is a pole next to the temple of Shiva, with a transformer resting on it and it is of no use at the moment. 'Ever since the Indians have stopped coming, they have become negligent again. The temple is falling into disrepair,' he says.

The boys have still not been able to set up the generator. One can hear the sound of its engine trying to start in the background. 'What's the problem? Does it have petrol?' asks a frustrated Diyal. 'It does. I don't know why it is not starting. There seems to be some problem with the engine. We will try again.'

Diyal has been upset ever since he heard the news about Bhatti's murder. In fact, he is the one who called Gupta. Being an activist, he had met the former minister several times. 'I had told him about this pilgrimage. He had assured me he would take care of everything,' says Diyal. His tone has changed now. There is a deep sadness in his voice which has replaced the fury. 'But then this happened. I cannot even call his secretary,' he adds. Besides activism, Diyal teaches comparative religion at Peshawar University. He holds a master's degree in Islamic studies. 'I believe that being a minority living in a Muslim state, it is imperative for us to learn about Islam. I urge all other members of the minority communities to do so,' he says. A lot of educated non-Muslims feel the same. The trend has gained momentum more so recently after archaic Islamic laws are used to persecute the members of religious minorities. The educated lot feel that if the members of the communities are better aware of Islam and its laws, they would be able to avoid the persecution that interpretation of Islamic laws brings with itself, sometimes.

***

The numbers of pilgrims has now increased manifold. All the buses have arrived and are parked on the road. There are about a thousand people. The restaurant has closed. But for a few, most of the devotees have gathered at the courtyard of the Archaeology Department office. A senior police official, the deputy superintendent of police (DSP), has arrived. His official jeep stands in the courtyard amongst the people. Gupta argues with him to open the hall of the department, so that at least the women, children and the elderly can rest. It is still drizzling. The DSP argues back saying that the Hindus had been told not to come here. He cites the security conditions of the country as his reason. He remains adamant that he cannot open the hall as he does not have jurisdiction over it. After a little while, Gupta is finally able to convince the DSP, who opens one of the halls of the building and allows a few pilgrims to rest inside. On Gupta's instructions, only the women, old and children are allowed inside, while a couple of young boys stand at the entrance stopping anyone else from going in. Young boys, looking for an opportunity to flirt with the girls inside, make random excuses to go into the hall. In front of the hall, on a small lawn, a group of boys set up a sound system. Bhajans blare out of them, while the boys dance in front. Next to the ground, in the courtyard, men start making arrangements for langar. Lentils will be cooked for dinner along with tea. Across the road, in the temple, the generator has failed to work. The innovative young technicians have taken a wire from the Archaeology Department office and lit one bulb in the complex. A few exhausted old men rest here, hiding under their blankets.

Standing next to a cauldron, Gupta is overseeing the food preparations. He is wearing a badge that his son was distributing to the pilgrims in order to be allowed access into the temple. All the pilgrims are wearing one. The celebration of Shivratri, which literally means the 'night of Shiva' includes the worship of Shiva throughout the night, as well as a symbolic marriage between him and his counterpart, Parvati. 'After langar, women will take the mehndi of Shiv to the temple, as sisters and sister-in-laws do so for the grooms,' Gupta explains. Mehndi is an important part of Pakistani marriages, during which the women apply henna on the hands of the groom and the bride. In this case, this will only be a symbolic gesture. However, there will also be real marriages during the Shivratri celebration. 'This is an auspicious night so we have organised four other marriages here. These are girls from Khyber Pakhtunkhwa and FATA (Federally Administered Tribal Areas), who suffered during the floods of 2010. Some of these girls cannot afford a proper marriage. A few lost their families during the catastrophe. The marriages have been organised by the contributions of the Sangat (the Hindu community present),' says Gupta.

Dinner is served at eleven in the night. Two white plastic

sheets are spread on the floor as pilgrims squat on them, while other young volunteers serve them. The children are put to sleep after dinner, while women set out to prepare for the breakfast. For some pilgrims, this meal will mark the start of their fast that they will then break at noon tomorrow, in lieu of the Shivratri festival.

Following the dinner, a musical band gathers in the courtyard, playing popular Indian songs on a trumpet, bass drum, crashes and other drums. They have also come from Peshawar. Boys, who were earlier dancing to the bhajans, gather around the band. Women go into the hall and bring out the mehndi that will be taken to the shrine. These are small decorated plates, containing oil lamps and lumps of henna. Another group of women take out a shawl and hold it up high, with four women holding the four corners. In a conventional wedding, the groom would walk under this, but since this is the wedding procession of Lord Shiva, there is no one standing underneath it. The group gathers in a procession, with the boys and the men dancing in front as the women follow. Leaving the department's courtyard, the procession steps out onto the road. It is deserted at this time of the night. The buses of the pilgrims stand in one corner, next to the ancient staircase leading up to the university. The procession comes to halt for a little while as the group decides to stop and dance. The boys drag in other men who had been watching from the corner. A few women also join them.

Inside the temple complex the procession moves towards the shrine of Lord Shiva, situated next to the pool. The floor is made of marble and is wet at the moment. Leading, the men enter first, taking their shoes off at the steps. The floor is cold, but motivated by religious fervour they are able to withstand it.

It is a small light brown building, with a small dome at the top. There is a wooden door, covered with floral decorations. In the centre of the room there is a phallic like structure, called the Shivling. This structure represents the potent force of Lord Shiva. It is a small room, which can only accommodate about ten people. Leading the group is Diyal. Elder women, holding aarti and mehndi, are allowed to enter. They place the mehndi plates at the base of the deity and perform the aarti. The band stands next to the threshold and continues to play, enhancing the festivities. There is a rush of people at the entrance, climbing over each others' shoulders to get a view of the proceedings inside.

A couple of men bring a container of milk. Holding the container with the help of another man, Diyal pours it onto the Shivling. This is an offering to the God by the devotees. Following this, all the devotees pray. This marks the conclusion of the ceremony. The women head back to the hall, whereas the men sleep wherever they find a place.

***

At about nine in the morning, the officials of the Archaeology Department, unaware of the situation, come to work. They find their offices invaded and the temples full of sleeping pilgrims. Across the road, the pilgrims are preparing for the festivities of the day. Traders are setting up their stalls by spreading out their wares on the roadside. These include small idols, pictures of deities, CDs of bhajan recordings, toys for children, bindiyas and mangalsutras. Unwilling to wait for everyone to wake up and vacate the hall, which the pilgrims were going to do in a couple of hours anyway, junior officials from the department enter the hall and start picking up their luggage and throwing it out into the courtyard. This causes a panic as the women shout and fight back. The officials refuse to listen to anyone. Another group picks up the utensils and other material used to prepare the langar, including rice, and throw it on the road.

Both Gupta and Diyal rush to the scene. Women sit at the foot of the hall beating their chests and wailing. Others try to rescue their bags from the officials. Some are picking up their clothes from the floor. Diyal asks the boys to pick up the utensils and eatables from the road and put them inside the temple. Gupta tries to argue with the officials to allow them to vacate peacefully; Diyal makes a few frenzied calls to his friends in the media. He wants to use the threat of media to placate the officials.

***

It has been an hour since the officials threw out the devotees and there is still no sign of the media. The pilgrims, who were not able to explore the temple yesterday, are wandering around. A few are having their photographs taken next to the pool. It is too cold to take a bath so they enjoy its scenic beauty instead. A few take some water from the pond in their hands and pour it on their heads. This is a substitute to performing a ritual ablution or 'ashnan'. Children are playing with the toys that they have bought from the stalls. Diyal tries to call his friends in the media again, but nobody responds. The officials have cleaned the hall and are at work there now. Unlike the previous day, it is a sunny day, perfect for the pilgrims to enjoy themselves in the open.

(Extracted from *A White Trail* by Haroon Khalid, Westland, 2013)

Frolicking Among Deer: A Short History of Pashupati

Amish Raj Mulmi

For Nepalis of a certain age, Pashupati carries with it the royal baggage of being Nepal's tutelary deity. In the early years of the twenty-first century, when the Maoist insurgency was at its peak, a dour-looking King Gyanendra would end his televised public addresses by invoking the protection of Lord Pashupatinath—'*Pashupatinath le hami sabaiko rakshya garun*!' (May Pashupatinath protect us all). Earlier kings, similarly, invoked the deity's protection over the kingdom. Such national veneration continues even in republican Nepal. The lord of animals (the literal meaning of Pashupatinath) has been, since at least the seventh century CE onwards, the keeper of Nepal, the god of the ruling class, and the heart of a country that was once intended to be an 'asal hindu-sthan' (a 'pure' Hindu nation).

In the seventh century CE, the Licchavi Mahasamant Amshuverman (reigned 595–621 CE) issued 'prashastis' or proclamations in which he claimed to be 'favoured by the feet of Pashupati': '*bhagavat-Pasupati-bhattaraka-padanugrhitah*'.[1] He was perhaps the first ruler of Kathmandu to anoint himself with Pashupati's divine blessings. The worship of Pashupati—and the divine status of Devpatan, the Kathmandu locality in which the temple is located, including the holy forest of Mrigasthali—long predate Amshuverman's panegyrics, however. While little is known about the connections between the Indus Valley seal that is said to depict a seated lord of the animals and the Pashupati shrine itself, the deity is at the centre of what makes Kathmandu Valley holy. It is a 'tirtha' (a holy spot) at par with the greatest of Hindu pilgrimage sites; an axis mundi that turns sacred everything it touches; a cremation site that promises instant salvation to those who are burnt by the ghats of the Bagmati river; and crucial to the identity of Nepal as an imagined 'Hindu rashtra'.

***

'First of all there was nothing in Nepal except Pashupatinath, whose beginning and end none can know or tell.'[2] Thus, as the Brahminical chronicles of Nepal say, did Nepal come into existence. The origin stories of Pashupati are many. The Lord Shiva grew tired of the Banaras gods' incessant adulation, and retired to the Shlesmantak forest across the Pashupati temple having assumed the form of a gazelle, where the gods seized him by the horn, which broke and resulted in three different shrines on three different planets. 'Siva declared, "Since I have dwelt in the Slesmantaka wood in the form of a beast (pasu), therefore throughout the universe my name shall be Pasupati."'[3] Another variant of the myth states that Shiva and Parvati frolicked in the woods of Shlesmantak as gazelles, and when the gods discovered him there and tried to take him back to Banaras, 'he leapt to the other side of the Bagmati, where his horn broke into four pieces, after which he manifested as Pasupati in a four-faced (caturmukha) linga.'[4]

In another version, the Goddess Sati threw herself into the fire when her father Daksa Prajapati insulted Shiva, her husband. The god sunk into depression and carried her body across the universe. In Guhyeswori, the shrine to the east of Pashupati, fell her genitals. 'This same Guhya Devi was born as daughter to [the] Rajah [of] Himachal and was given in marriage to Mahadeva with the country of Nepal as her dowry. The Rajah also gave the bride and bridegroom Himachal Desh and sent them to Pasupatipura, where the august pair or *Visva-Sakti* took for their lodging a place called Mrigasthali.'[5]

The Pashupati shrine is also regarded as an earthly manifestation of the jyotirlinga, the infinite ray of light Brahma and Vishnu sought to discover the ends of. The shrine has been identified as 'Maheshwarpur' in the Mahabharata.[6] Another myth, as recalled to me in the Garhwal Himalayas, suggests that after the Kurukshetra war, when the Pandavas desired to meet Shiva to purge them of the sins of killing their kin, the god was in no mood to do so and tried to escape, burrowing into the earth as a bull. When the mighty Bhima caught the bull by the tail, the rump manifested itself in Kedar, while the head emerged in Pashupati (and the other appendages manifested themselves as the Panch-Kedar shrines).

Nonetheless, all of these are said to have occurred in the age of the gods. In time, the shrine crumbled and disappeared, buried under the weight of man's sins in Kaliyug. Then, a cow belonging to a herder named Nep—in some versions, the herder is named Gopala—would go to the site where Pashupati lay hidden, and pour milk over it. The curious herder unearthed the linga, and established a temple, which was the first of the Pashupati temples.[7] Local chronicles also suggest the first Pashupati temple was built either by Pasupreksa of the Somadeva dynasty in the third century BCE, or by Supuspadeva, a Licchavi king who is said to have ruled thirty-nine generations before his descendant Manadeva in the fifth century CE, one of Kathmandu Valley's first recorded rulers. Both Pasupreksa and Supuspadeva have not left many historical records.[8] Records suggest the medieval era king Shivdev, who ruled in the twelfth century, had possibly rebuilt the temple, and given it a copper roof.[9] But we reach firmer historical ground in the thirteenth century, when king Ananta Malla had the temple renovated and the roof gilded. In the fourteenth century, the temple suffered under the iconoclasm of Bengal sultan Shamsuddin, who is said to have broken the original linga in three pieces and sacked the temple, following which king Jayasinghramvardhan rebuilt the temple. The history of the shrine then becomes a history of royal bequests; successive kings, queens and courtiers embellished the temple over time, until the current three-tiered pagoda structure was built from the ground up in the reign of Bhupalendra Malla in the late seventeenth century.[10] Pashupati imitations have been founded in Bhaktapur and Patan, and in Banaras, where it is simply known as the Nepali temple, and was constructed by the Shah king Ran Bahadur in the early years of the nineteenth century.

That the Pashupati complex has long been a site of supreme religious importance is borne not by the Pashupati shrine itself, but another linga called the Ratnesvara linga in the Pashupati 'kshetra' (realm), which was enshrined in 477 CE by a merchant named Ratnasangha and is the oldest among the Shaivite shrines in Pashupati.[11] The oldest reference to Pashupati himself comes from the Bhasmesvara linga, established in 533 CE in

'Lord Pashupati's realm (kshetra)'.[12] Several other lingas from this period can be found in the complex even today, giving rise to the belief that Shaivism was widespread and practised by the elite at the time, and 'emerge[d] as a powerful alternative to Vaiṣṇavism as a royal religion'.[13]

***

No other Hindu deity in South Asia has come to be so closely associated with the ruling class as Pashupati. Votive lingas, or lingas consecrated by the ruling class and the elite, can be found scattered among the temple complex, despite possessing 'scarcely any ritual function'.[14] Several of the lingas, like the Ratnesvara cited above, date back to Licchavi times; but a majority of them were placed from the middle of the eighteenth century onwards, when the Shah kings and the Rana prime ministers asserted their rule over Nepal Valley, and subsequently, the rest of the country.

Jung Bahadur, the first Rana prime minister, built the Visvarupa temple complex in 1864 inside the Mrigasthali forest, which remains closed after the 2015 earthquake. Similarly, the Vasuki temple dedicated to the king of the Nagas was built by Pratap Malla in the seventeenth century. There are other shrines to the various ganas of Shiva: the Bhairavs, Ganesh, and the massive bronze Nandi statue that guards the western gates of the Pashupati temple and was established by Jagat Jung, Jung Bahadur's oldest son and the tragic hero of the classic Nepali novel *Seto Bagh* (White Tiger).[15] There are also several shrines associated with Vishnu, including the oldest Vishnu statue in all of Kathmandu Valley that has been dated to 467 CE but today lies outside the temple complex,[16] and a few associated with Buddhism as well. A most curious icon is of Virupaksa, which has 'tribal facial features' and is 'distinctly pre-Hindu in nature', with a host of myths associated with the half-buried statue that is enshrined in a small temple next to the royal cremation ghat.[17] Although the chronicles relate a different origin story for Virupaksa, a popular myth regards the deity as the herald of the end of Kaliyug, emerging fully only when this age will collapse.

But it is the goddesses of Pashupati that are 'both in part companions of the great gods and, to some extent, independent and potentially dangerous'.[18] Most of these goddesses—among them Vatsala, to whom Devpatan's most significant festival is dedicated, and Guhyeshwari—are worshipped with animal sacrifices and alcohol, in direct contrast to the sattvik methods of worship dedicated to Pashupati, with the rituals indicating conflicts between different traditions and the gods themselves. These goddesses are both local and expansive; the Vatsala festival incorporates several of Kathmandu's shakti shrines within its annual passage across Kathmandu, while the Guhyeshwari shrine is important to both Buddhists and Hindus.

As a sacred complex, Pashupati's history is equally mired in the tussles between various Hindu sects that are manifested in the contest between the god and the female deities, and between Buddhism and Shaivite Hinduism itself.[19] As the story goes, in the reign of Vriksadevavarma, a Licchavi king said to rule around 400 CE, the Buddhists had the upper hand in Pashupati, and 'used to throw leavings of their food and drink on Pashupatinath every evening and that next morning remove it from his image and worship it'.[20] The Shaivites were defeated via debate and driven out of the country. It fell up to

Shankaracharya to come to Nepal and defeat the Buddhists, first by releasing the Goddess Saraswati whom the Buddhists had trapped in a jar and thus defeated the Shaivites previously, and second, by overpowering 'the Buddhamargis by his warm and powerful eloquence'.

While popular versions equate the Shankaracharya in this tale with the eighth century Shaivite revivalist, it is quite unlikely that Adi Shankara indeed visited Nepal. Although there is a Shankaracharya math (monastery) within the Pashupati complex, there isn't any evidence to suggest the math was set up by Adi Shankara.[21] However, the tale does point to a larger contest between Buddhists and Shaivites over control of Pashupati; there is historical evidence to suggest Narendradeva, a seventh century Licchavi king, gave land to Buddhist monks within the temple complex.[22] Further, Buddhist chronicles about Nepal record the monk Krakuchchanda telling his pupils, 'In this lovely grove [i.e. Mrigasthali] eminent Siddhas, Yogis, Devatas will hereafter settle, and then this grove will be a sanctuary. Behold now how in order to worship Sri Guhjesvari, the three Deities—Brahma, Vishnu and Mahesa—have assumed the likeness of deer and are running about. Know further that a Linga of Mahadeva will appear here and this grove will be named Mrgasthali.'[23]

Such chronicles and blurred pasts suggest that the Buddhists indeed had a role to play within Devpatan. Slusser wrote Buddhist priests had influence in the shrine until the sixteenth century. On the day of Kartik Shukla Ashtami, known as 'mukhastami', the Pashupati linga was 'adorned with a Bodhisattva crown', and Buddhists were permitted to worship Pashupati in the guise of Avalokitesvara. Slusser, however, noted this practice was in the decline, and in the present, the shrine has come to be a solely Shaivite one.[24]

The advent of Pashupati, however, as a royal deity—or, in other words, the preferred god among Nepal's ruling class—seems to follow Amshuverman's declarations of allegiance to the shrine. Although commonly stated that all kings of Nepal thereafter followed suit, as scholar Nina Mirnig argues, '[t]he popularisation of Pashupati coincides with a period when the Licchavi kings were temporarily supplanted by their royal officials [just as Amshuverman was], and it is through this role as a symbol of power independent of the royal house that Pashupati may have been successfully linked to the ruling elite of Nepal'.[25] Further, the linkages between the Pashupata sect of Shaivism and the Pashupati temple itself cannot be ignored, especially since these links became all the more stronger during the Licchavi period when the shrine itself began to be adopted as a tutelary deity. 'Saivism's emergence in Nepal is often described as almost directly linked to the presence of Pasupatas',[26] with five seventh century inscriptions explicitly mentioning the sect.

Subsequently, while the Malla kings held the Taleju goddess as their royal deity, Pashupati was never too far from their minds, as can be seen by the many grants, constructions and renovations to the temple complex. Pashupati was a site not just for royal obeisance, but also of propitiation, as the king Pratap Malla did, 'during which time he erected numerous lingas and a temple, performed lavish sacrifices, including kotyahuti and tuladana, and gave gifts of all kinds to Pasupati'.[27] Another copper-plate document issued by eighteenth century Malla king Jayaprakash invokes various deities as witnesses before listing out what one can and cannot do in the shrines of Kathmandu, including the ruling that '[n]o one may even pluck leaves from trees at Mrgasthali'.[28]

The Shahs from Gorkha began to rule Nepal Valley from 1769 CE onwards, and as rulers of Kathmandu, came to adopt the regnal duties due to the shrine. In 1812, the rajpurohit (royal priest) Radhaballav Arjyal died without fulfilling his wish to donate silver doors to the shrine; by the next year, his followers had collected adequate monies to gift a silver door to the inner western gates of the shrine.[29] The kings, and other members of the royal family weren't far behind. Pashupati was the centre of royal adulation, penance and authority. The third Shah king Ran Bahadur Shah's reign was marked by political instability directly arising out of his third marriage to Kantabati, a Maithili Brahmin widow, who was visiting Kathmandu on a pilgrimage to Pashupati.[30] When Kantabati became afflicted with tuberculosis in 1798, Ran Bahadur abdicated the throne in favour of their two-year-old son Girvana Yuddha, assumed the name of Swami Nirgunanda, and went to live in Devpatan, where he gifted the shrine an expansive garden. 'Thirty-two houses were demolished to make room for the gardens, but compensation was given for them.'[31] In 1814, as tensions rose between the East India Company and the Gorkhalis, General Amar Singh Thapa offered silver doors to the northern gate of the shrine, embellished with the names of Nepal's sixty-four shivlingas and Thapa's family's images.[32] 'The most astonishing gift of all', as Slusser wrote, was by the king Rajendra Vikram Shah, who offered 125,000 oranges to the shrine in 1829 (although he did offer other gifts too).

The Ranas, who took over power from the Shahs from the middle of the nineteenth century onwards, equally endowed the temple complex with votive shrines across the Bagmati in the Mrigasthali forest. The series of similar looking shrines on the banks of the Bagmati directly across from the Pashupati temple itself were consecrated by Rana noblewomen in the aftermath of the infamous 1846 Kot Massacre that brought the Ranas to power.[33] Several other shrines include the name of the benefactor in their title, such as Chandraprakasesvara and Chandramuktesvara (both built by Rana prime minister Chandra Shamsher in 1903 and 1934 respectively).

Such beneficence continued into the modern era. The preamble to the 1948 Government of Nepal Act, the country's first constitution, explicitly recognised Nepal as 'this sacred country of Lord Pashupatinath', tying the deity to the Nepali state itself. Pashupati was both Nepal's primary deity as well as a symbol of the modern Nepali state, which was imagined as an asal Hindu-sthan in response to the Mughal and subsequently British rule over the subcontinent. The purity of the state thus became an immutable idea with the ruling class. As Jung Bahadur, the first Rana prime minister, noted in the preface to the 1866 law on religious endowments: 'We have our own country, a Hindu kingdom, where the law prescribes that "cows shall not be slaughtered", nor women and Brahmins sentenced to capital punishment; a holy land where the Himalayas, the Basuki Ksetra, the Arya tirtha, and the refulgent Sri Pasupati Linga and Sri Guhyesvari Pitha are located. In this Kali Age this is the only country in which Hindus rule.'[34]

***

The idea that the Pashupati shrine is a symbol of 'Hindu' Nepal has been reaffirmed not just historically, but also in the modern era, including in republican Nepal. This has often led to a contest between the traditions Pashupati espouses, and how modern Nepali politicians have interpreted these traditions. Within a few months of the appointment of the Nepal republic's first elected government in 2009, under the then-Maoists headed by Pushpa Kamal Dahal 'Prachanda', the temple turned into a site of conflict that arose out of the government's decision to appoint Nepali priests in lieu of the Indian priests who have traditionally headed the shrine.

Beyond such temporal contests, the Pashupati shrine is also where Indian diplomacy in Nepal finds its cultural anchor. One only needs to recall Indian prime minister Narendra Modi's 2014 visit to Pashupati, where he offered 2,500 kgs of sandalwood and a grant of Rs 25 crore to build a dharamshala on the temple grounds. The symbolism of a saffron-wearing Modi at Nepal's primary Hindu site of worship was also not missed. Further, Indian leaders and diplomats have often recalled the 'Pashupati-Tirupati' or other similar connections (as an example of shared religions) in defining the 'special' ties between the two countries, most recently by defence minister Rajnath Singh in the aftermath of the 2020 territorial dispute when he said, 'Who can forget Baba Pashupatinath? How can he be separated from Baba Amarnath, Somnath and Kashi Vishwanath? This relation is not from this world but a totally another world.'[35]

Indian pilgrims and religious leaders have long had a historic connection with the shrine. There are records of Indian pilgrims bequeathing gifts to the shrines from as early as the twelfth century.[36] Several Indian Hindu ascetic sects, such as the Dasnami and the Kanphata sects, have their own maths in the temple complex even today. The latter are the followers of Gorakhnath, the eleventh century ascetic, who is said to be the patron saint of the Shah dynasty, and whose most famous follower today is the Uttar Pradesh Chief Minister Yogi

Adityanath, who heads the Gorakhnath math in Gorakhpur. The Shankaracharya math at Pashupati, although popularly said to be founded by Adi Shankara, has hazier origins, with Tandon writing that it was a twelfth century ascetic who has been mentioned in edicts from the time as Shaivacharya, who founded the monastery. Shaivacharya is said to have visited Nepal twice, and had followers even among the royal family.[37]

The most prominent 'Indians' at the shrine since the eighteenth century have been the 'bhattas', the chief priests who are the only ones allowed to worship the linga directly and touch it. These bhattas are Dravidian Tailangi priests from the Smarta sect. Although when such Brahmins were first invited to conduct the worship is 'difficult to determine'[38]—one doubtful inscription dates back to the twelfth century—the first recorded instance comes from a 1735 CE document issued under the reign of Jagajjaya Malla.[39] The 'bhandaris' who assist the bhattas and also act as treasurers must, however, be Newar Shresthas from Devpatan itself. 'In other words, and seen from the sanctum: the insiders, the Bhattas, must come from the outside, and the outsiders, the Bhandaris, must come from the inside, i.e. Deopatan.'[40]

It was the Maoist revoking of the Dravidian priests' traditional authority, which was to be replaced by Nepali priests, that brought conflict to the shrine in the new republic. The Indian priests were attacked by Maoist cadres in two separate incidents in January and September 2009, while the decision to revoke traditional worship rights was met by widespread condemnation from groups such as the Vishva Hindu Parishad and the former Nepal king Gyanendra. Although the order was withdrawn, '[s]ome looked upon the replacement of the abbots as … evidence of an anti-India agenda; others as an attempt to whip up Nepali nationalism; while others thought it was the lucre-dakshina offerings that Pashupatinath received from Indian pilgrims in particular that explained it all. Still others perceived it as an attack on religion itself, and possibly part of deeper communist designs.'[41]

These disparate outlooks must be regarded against the dichotomy that has been apparent in republic Nepal's turn to secularism and the old pillars of the Hindu Nepali state. Among the demands of the Maoists when they came into the political mainstream was the adoption of secularism, a move that has long been decried by those opposed to it as a 'western import'. Backlash against the anti-federal movement resulted in a reimagination of what secularism would come to mean in the new republic. While the 2015 constitution incorporated Nepal as a secular state, it explicitly defined secularism as 'protection of religion and culture being practiced since ancient times and religious and cultural freedom', a watered-down version that retains the primacy of Brahmanism as has been practised in the country.

Thus, what we have in Nepal today is a situation where the president worships at Pashupati on Mahashivaratri as the head of state. But the question remains: What if Nepal gets a non-Hindu head of state in the future? Would the head of state then be allowed to carry out the same religious activities, especially as non-Hindus are prohibited inside the main complex even today? Further, as Nepal dove into political instability following a split in the ruling party in 2020, Prime Minister K.P. Oli's widely publicised visit to Pashupati—which was marked by an offering of 125,000 lamps, a gift of NRs 30 crores, and the promise to install a 'jalahari', or the vessel that drips milk or water from above the lingam, of 141 kgs of gold[42]—was also seen as an attempt to reach out to those who believe in the

Nepali Hindu state, especially at a time when several protests demanding the reinstatement of the monarchy and the Hindu state had been organised.[43]

That Pashupati is a site contested not just by the deities within its sacred enclosures, but also by the many mortals who each lay claim to the shrine in their own ways, only goes to suggest how pervasive, and intrinsic, the shrine is to Nepal. Previously, it was a seat of power that provided divine authority to those who ruled Kathmandu, and subsequently, Nepal. Today, it is a shrine that is contested at many levels, but the political symbolism behind its veneration has never truly gone away. Further, as social movements against caste grew against the backdrop of the 1950 revolution, nearly 1,100 Dalits attempted to enter the temple in 1954 in a most remarkable challenge to the existing Brahmin orthopraxy. '[T]he pressure created by this movement forced the government and "upper" caste locals to remove the signboard at the Pashupatinath temple that had proclaimed "Untouchables are Prohibited".'[44] However, even till date, non-Hindus cannot enter the temple complex, and can only view the shrine from across the Bagmati.

The status of Pashupati as Nepal's primary Hindu deity has remained unchallenged since at least the seventh century CE, and perhaps earlier, if one believes the local vamshavalis (chronicles) that trace the shrine back to the Satya Yug.[45] The deity itself has been venerated, patronised and co-opted by those who rule Nepal in various ways through history. In death, as in life, the shrine stands taller and has no other equal in Nepal; for those who believe in it, it ranks higher than even Banaras, the city of Shiva himself. For was it not the jungles of Mrigasthali that Shiva himself chose to retire to, and frolicked among the deer with his beloved Parvati!

Bibliography

Mary Slusser, *Nepal Mandala: A Cultural Study of the Kathmandu valley,* Vol. 1, Princeton University Press, Princeton: 1982

Bikrama Jit Hasrat, *History of Nepal As Told by its Own and Contemporary Chroniclers*, V.V. Research Institute Press, Hoshiarpur, Punjab: 1970

Axel Michaels, *Siva in Trouble: Festivals and Rituals at the Pasupatinatha Temple of Deopatan*, Oxford University Press, New York: 2008

Dr Govind Tandon, *Itihas ka Thap Pristh Haru* (History's Additional Pages), Sangrila Books, Kathmandu: 2019

Nina Mirnig, 'Favoured by the Venerable Lord Paśupati: Tracing the Rise of a New Tutelary Deity in Epigraphic Expressions of Power in Early Medieval Nepal', *Indo-Iranian Journal 56*, No. 3/4 (2013): 325-47

Nina Mirnig, 'Early Strata of Śaivism in the Kathmandu Valley', *Indo-Iranian Journal 59*, No. 4 (2016): 309-62,

Notes

1 Mary Slusser, *Nepal Mandala: A Cultural Study of the Kathmandu Valley,* Vol. 1, Princeton University Press, Princeton: 1982, p. 228

2 Bikrama Jit Hasrat, *History of Nepal As Told by its Own and Contemporary Chroniclers*, V.V. Research Institute Press, Hoshiarpur, Punjab: 1970, p. 23

3 Slusser, op cit., p. 226

4 Axel Michaels, *Siva in Trouble: Festivals and Rituals at the Pasupatinatha Temple of Deopatan*, Oxford University Press, New York: 2008, p. 11

5 Hasrat, op cit., p. 23

6 Dr Govind Tandon, *Itihas ka Thap Pristh Haru* (History's Additional Pages), Sangrila Books, Kathmandu: 2019, p. 6

7 Hasrat, op cit., p. 33 and Tandon, op cit., p. 5

8 Michaels, op cit., p. 10
9 Tandon, op cit., p. 8
10 Ibid, pp. 8-9
11 Nina Mirnig, 'Early Strata of Śaivism in the Kathmandu Valley', *Indo-Iranian Journal 59,* No. 4 (2016): 309-362, doi: https://doi.org/10.1163/15728536-05904001
12 Slusser, op cit., p. 227
13 Mirnig, 'Early Strata of Saivism'
14 Michaels, op cit., p. 11
15 Tandon, op cit., p. 8
16 Michaels, op cit., p. 15
17 Ibid
18 Ibid
19 For more on the contest between Pashupati and the goddesses, see Michaels, *Siva in Trouble.*
20 Hasrat, op cit., p. 38
21 See Tandon for more on this debate.
22 Michaels, op cit., p. 19
23 Hasrat, op cit., p. xxi
24 Slusser, op cit., p. 227
25 Nina Mirnig, 'Favoured by the Venerable Lord Paśupati: Tracing the Rise of a New Tutelary Deity in Epigraphic Expressions of Power in Early Medieval Nepal.' *Indo-Iranian Journal 56,* No. 3/4 (2013): 325-47. Accessed 4 February 2021, http://www.jstor.org/stable/24665987
26 Mirnig, 'Early Strata of Saivism'
27 Slusser, op cit., p. 231
28 Ed. and trans. Bal Gopal Shrestha with Ramhari Timalsina and Manik Bajracharya, 'A copper-plate decree of King Jayaprakāśa Malla prohibiting certain activities in various shrines of Kathmandu (NS 872)', Heidelberg Academy of Sciences and Humanities: Documents on the History of Religion and Law of Pre-modern Nepal, Heidelberg, Germany, 2017, courtesy of the National Archives,

Kathmandu, https://abhilekha.adw.uni-heidelberg.de/nepal/editions/show/16791

29 Tandon, op cit., p. 11

30 Amish Raj Mulmi, 'Swami Nirgunanda: The Monk who would have given his Kingdom away', *The Wire*, 1 July 2017, https://thewire.in/history/swami-nirgunanda-the-monk-who-would-have-given-his-kingdom-away

31 Munshi Shew Shankar Singh and Pandit Shri Gunanand (ed. Daniel Wright), *History of Nepal with an Introductory Sketch of the Country and People of Nepal*, Cambridge University Press, Cambridge: 1877, p. 262

32 Tandon, op cit., p. 11

33 Michaels, op cit., p. 11

34 M.C. Regmi, 'Guthi Legislation in the 1866 Legal Code', Regmi Research Series, Vol. 4, December 1972, p. 101. Also see Richard Burghart, 'The Formation of the Concept of Nation-State in Nepal', *The Journal of Asian Studies 44*, No. 1 (1984) for more on the Hindu foundations of the Nepali state

35 Kalyan Das, '"How can India-Nepal ties break?" in Rajnath Singh's speech references to Gorkhas and spiritual connect', *Hindustan Times,* 15 July 2020

36 Tandon, op cit., p. 19

37 Tandon, op cit., pp. 49-50

38 Michaels, op cit., p. 21

39 Ibid. Also Tandon, op cit., p. 21

40 Michaels, op cit., p. 24

41 Rakesh Shukla, 'The Commissar and the Priest', *Himal Southasia*, 10 February 2009, https://www.himalmag.com/the-commissar-and-the-priest/

42 Kedar Dahal, 'Pashupatima 141 kilo sunko jalari rakhne nirnaya' (Pashupati to be granted a 141-kg gold vessel), *Naya Patrika*, 1 February 2021, https://www.nayapatrikadaily.com/news-details/59424/2021-02-01

43 Bhadra Sharma, 'The Prime Minister finds his religion', *The Record*, 31 January 2021, https://www.recordnepal.com/wire/features/the-prime-minister-finds-his-religion/

44 Ashwini K.P., 'Pashupatinath Temple Entry Movement', *Dalit History Month*, 7 April 2019, https://dalithistorymonth.medium.com/pashupatinath-temple-entry-movement-dalit-assertion-in-nepal-eeee07623cb4

45 The Satya Yuga is a mythological measure of time in Hinduism. It is the first of the four yugas (world ages) in a yuga cycle, preceded by the Kaliyuga of the previous cycle and followed by Treta Yuga. Satya Yuga is known as the age of truth, when humanity is governed by gods, and every manifestation is close to its purest ideal. The Satya Yuga was said to last for 1,728,000 years.

The Icon of Jaffna

Thulasi Muttulingam

Adoration of Lord Murugan is deeply enmeshed in the Sri Lankan psyche—among the indigenous Veddhas, the Sinhalese and Tamils alike. The ever-youthful divine princeling is a much loved deity on these shores. Particularly as he's supposed to have wed a Sri Lankan indigenous girl, Valli, a Veddha chieftain's daughter. In Sinhala Buddhism, he's a much loved guardian deity of the island nation. In Tamil Hinduism, he's an accessible Adonis who settled down with a local girl. The local girl being an indigenous Veddha, the Veddha community worship him too and run one of the most important shrines to him in the country in the hilly, forested terrain of Kataragama, Sri Lanka. Alongside Kataragama which draws pilgrims on pada yatra (foot pilgrimage) from around the country, there are many other shrines to the resplendent princeling dotting the island. The Tamil enclave of Jaffna has its fair share of well-known Murugan shrines too.

Of these, one of the most well-known identity markers of Jaffna, widely used by the Sri Lanka Tourism Promotion Bureau as an emblem of the region, is the Nallur Kandaswamy Temple. It shows up well in promotional photos with its unique façade and is thus a well-known feature in Jaffna postcards.

People from around the world familiar with the area or who have visited it even once recognise the famed iconic temple instantly. It's a beacon to millions with its Tamil-lettered 'Om Muruga' flashing gopuram at its main entrance ushering in the faithful and the culturally curious alike, from both local and international shores. In the heart of Jaffna city, surrounded by pristine white sands and an ever-elaborately evolving temple structure, adored by millions, Lord Murugan reigns supreme.

Jaffna is often associated with Sri Lanka's long drawn-out civil war. Even now, a decade past the end of that thirty-year war, that's what the area is best known for outside its own environs. Perhaps fitting then that its most iconic deity is the Hindu god of war. Locally, however, he's known more as a lover than a warrior. So much so that he became immortalised by the Liberation Tigers of Tamil Eelam (LTTE) in one of their promotional songs for seemingly all the wrong reasons—as per the LTTE anyway. They critiqued him for cavorting with Valli instead of lending his support to their cause. It might well have been an oblique reference to the temple management keeping well clear of politics and the ethnicised conflict. Nevertheless, Lord Murugan isn't held by his adoring Tamil public to have taken part in the war. His adoring Sinhala public don't think he took partisan sides in it either. Vishnu, on the other hand, is held to have done that (on the side of the Sinhalese), but that's another story.

Skanda/Murugan in the meantime is worshipped all over Sri Lanka as a cherubic mischievous child, a handsome and stylish prince, a romantic prankster lover but not as a god of war. Every November, for the Kanda Shasti festival which celebrates the main events in the life of this god, the Sooran Por (his famous war against the asura king Soorapadman) is enacted—but the people are much more invested in his subsequent romance with Valli on Sri Lankan shores and the placation of the first wife Deivayani directly after when he comes home with his second wife. Bigamy for an ordinary man would be frowned upon but Murugan returning to his palace with his local conquest to find the doors locked to him by the first wife gains him a lot of sympathy—every year there is much investment in his long drawn-out romance and ultimate conjugal bliss with both wives after sending emissaries including finally Lord Vishnu to placate his first wife.

And that's how he's widely worshipped around the nation here. The handsome god astride a peacock, with a light-skinned wife, the Goddess Deivayani on his right and the dark-skinned tribal wife, the Goddess Valli on his left. In Nallur though, he's worshipped symbolically as a 'vel' (his spear). His physical form is absent.[1] This carries with it its own history and an ongoing feud on agamic versus non-agamic worship forms culturally cleaving as well as entrenching the temple's foremost place in Jaffna Tamils' consciousness.

History of the temple

Nallur Kandaswamy Temple is believed by Jaffna's Tamils to be one their most historic temples. They trace it back a thousand years or more via popular imagination. The current edifice, however, dates back to 1736. It was built to commemorate the historical memory of the ancient temple that people remembered via popular folklore as once standing in the vicinity. At the time the current temple was built, Jaffna was under Dutch rule and all its temples had been razed to the ground more than a century earlier by the invading Portuguese, in 1620.

All precolonial religious structures had long been demolished by that time and Catholicism under the Portuguese and later, Calvinism under the Dutch had been forced upon the people. Popular folkloric memory is still rampant with tales of how people secretly continued to worship their Hindu gods. Symbolism took the place of statues, and so trident and vel worship became common among the masses—stuck under trees and explained away as gardening tools to the colonisers.

Towards the end of the Dutch period (the late 1730s), however, the governors became a little more lenient in allowing the locals to worship their own gods. The Dutch governor's wife had favoured one of the neighbourhood children, and brought him up as a protégé at the Dutch fortress. When he grew up and wished to build a Shiva temple, he was given permission—although being the first temple of its kind, it had to be slowly opened up for public worship. Permission had originally been granted to only keep it as part of his residence. Then he sought permission for friends and family to visit the temple and then went on to make it public. This was Vaithilinga Chettiar whose descendants still run the Vannarpannai Sivan Kovil, now a protected monument of Sri Lanka. Once that temple began to go public, a shroff (accountant) in the Dutch administrative service, Maapana Mudaliyar, sought permission to rebuild the historic Nallur Kandaswamy Temple as well.

The ideation and veneration for that temple was still strong in folk memory but its exact precolonial location had by then been forgotten. Based on approximations of folk memory, Mudaliyar had selected a region in the general area of the old Nallur kingdom—which had been a Muslim settlement till just a few years prior—and placed a vel with a small edifice there. The original structure was quite humble, made of stone and a cadjan roof. The building of these two temples marked the beginning of Hindu revivalism in the region which had been at least nominally Christian under threat of the sword for over a century.

Current scholarship estimates the original Nallur temple's location to be where an Anglican St James Church is currently standing, about a hundred metres away. It was originally a Catholic church under the Portuguese, then a Calvinist church under the Dutch and eventually became an Anglican church under the British, which still stands. Roadwork in the 1970s led to the discovery of underlying structures in this area, leading scholars to estimate it to be the likely site of the original Nallur Kandaswamy Temple.

As of now, three major religions are united in the quest for the historical Nallur—and settle their differences amicably and even respectfully. The church is held to be the site of the original temple, and the current temple is situated amidst an old Muslim settlement, adjoining a Sufi tomb worshipped until recently by Muslims. Nevertheless, due to the decades-long war, there is wariness in discussing what is well-known historical as well as current memory, in case it broils over into religious or ethnic conflict.

The current temple, now possibly in its fifth avatar, is built upon a historical memory of a kingly seat that was sacked several times and then rebuilt in both precolonial and colonial history.

The earliest references to the temple within Sri Lanka are from Sinhalese sources, *Rajavaliya* and *Kokila Sandesa*, dating to the fifteenth and seventeenth centuries. They refer to a Sapumal Kumaraya, who later ruled the country from the Kotte kingdom as King Buvaneka Bahu VI. He marched into Jaffna in 1450 to sack the kingdom there run by Tamil chieftains and then ruled over their kingdom over the next seventeen years. As such, he is said to have sacked their capital city Nallur, then rebuilt it along with the Nallur Kandaswamy Temple—the Sinhalese sources are not clear on whether he was responsible for rebuilding an existing temple that he had sacked, or built a new one.

When the Portuguese, a few centuries, later destroyed the area's temples, they used the dismantled stones to build their fort on the coast, which still stands. Archaeological research around this fort in 1971 yielded a stone with an inscription from Rajendra Chola dated to 1030 CE, recording his contributions to a temple in the area of Nallur, but it does not specify whether it was the Nallur Kandaswamy Temple. Scholars estimate it likely could have been as it was the most important temple for kings of the area—including when they invaded, as in the case of Rajendra Chola. Nallur was the capital city of Jaffna kingdom and the Kandaswamy Temple the primary temple worshipped by its sovereigns.

Since many of Jaffna's own records were destroyed during colonial rule—or else taken away to Portuguese and Dutch archives from where they are yet to be retrieved—apart from this stone inscription found in Jaffna, Sinhalese and Tamil historical documents written in the fifteenth to seventeenth centuries are the only available documents tracing the temple's history at the moment. The Sinhalese sources predating currently available Tamil sources attributing the building of the temple to King Buvaneka Bahu can be a tetchy subject in the country. Like everything else, it has become ethnicised and politicised through a contemporary lens which does not reflect medieval Sri Lankan reality. The issue in contention is that if

King Buvaneka Bahu VI built the Nallur Kandaswamy Temple, it is of Sinhala origin and not Tamil.

King Buvaneka Bahu VI, however, was not Sinhalese. He was the adopted son of the previous king of Kotte, and various sources place him as either an East Sri Lankan Tamil or a Tamil mercenary from South India. He is known as Chempaka Perumal in Tamil sources, and Sapumal Kumaraya in Sinhala sources—Tamilised and Sinhalised versions of the same name based on the fragrant butter-coloured Magnolia champaca flower from which he drew his name. A seventeenth-century Sinhalese manuscript, the *Mukkara Hatana*, detailing the exploits of the Karava/Karaiyar caste who were once military mercenaries employed by Sri Lankan kings, claims him as one of their own. His father as per this document was a Tamil Karaiyar chief called Manikka Thalaivan who was killed in battle, and thus he came to be adopted by the reigning king of Kotte.

The Karaiyar/Karava caste of Sri Lanka claim kshatriya lineage from India. They were employed as mercenaries to guard the nation's maritime provinces by Sri Lankan kings. Therefore they were settled all along the coastline of the island nation, with those in Tamil-dominant areas becoming Tamilised and those in Sinhala-dominant areas becoming Sinhalised, known as the Karaiyar and Karava caste respectively. It is the same caste and they acknowledge kinship with each other across the ethnicised divide. Today, many are fishermen as the advent of colonialism took away their military role but they still remember their military background of defending the country with pride.

Closer to the present day, the Karaiyar community predominated in the LTTE, and harked back to their militant past and valour to explain the phenomenon. Likewise, the Sri Lankan army has a major representation of the Karava caste who too claim that their military past and might is reflected in the present. Both Prabakaran, the LTTE leader, and General Sarath Fonseka, the army commander who won the final war against the LTTE, are Karaiyar and Karava respectively. In other words, kin. Unfortunately, in modern-day Sri Lanka, history such as this is brushed under the carpet to demarcate strong ethnic divides which do not reflect reality. The history of the Nallur Kandaswamy Temple is just one more of these politicised issues in the country now. The current temple management however does credit Chempaka Perumal, as King Buvaneka Bahu VI is known here, as an original builder of the temple in their oral history, recited at every festival.

The kings who ruled Jaffna as an independent kingdom however and styled themselves the Arya Chakravarthis predated the advent of Buvaneka Bahu VI, and took over the reign of Jaffna again when he left seventeen years later to claim his kingdom at Kotte. They ruled from Nallur as before, with Nallur Kandaswamy Temple as their central shrine.

The well-known travellers of the medieval world, the Venetian Marco Polo and the Moroccan Ibn Batuta, have left records of an independent kingdom in Jaffna with an Arya Chakravarthi in power when they travelled through it in the thirteenth and fourteenth centuries respectively. Since Jaffna kingdom's history is hotly disputed even now within the framework of the ethnicised conflict ravaging Sri Lanka, not much independent research has been done on it.

Many of Jaffna's own records disappeared during its five hundred-year history of colonial rule. Academics from Jaffna University now believe that many records might be found in

Portuguese or Dutch archives of the time period but while some work has been done drawing from English colonial sources, not much effort has yet been made to extract it from the previous colonial sources of the Dutch and the Portuguese. Nevertheless, we do know that a Portuguese writer called Queroze wrote of the existence of the Nallur Kandaswamy Temple before its sacking by his compatriots.

Despite over five hundred years since the deposition and execution of the last king of Jaffna, Sangili II by the Portuguese, the place names around Nallur and its suburbs hark back to the kingdom. 'Panikkar Valavu', where the palace elephants were stabled, 'Ariyalai', where the horses were stabled, 'Arasadi' and 'Rasa Veethi', where the king took his walks, 'Sangiliayan Thoppu' and 'Rasavin Thottam',the king's gardens or parks, among many others are still extant place names in and around the Nallur vicinity.

As a densely populated area, not many archaeological surveys have been done, but Jaffna archaeologists point out remote sensory equipment would likely yield a lot of information given that just digging a little below the soil in farm lands dotting the area yield potsherds and coins of a much earlier era. Despite this, not much in the nature of archaeological surveys have taken place. A road construction in the 1970s yielded many artefacts but with the ethnic conflict then heating up, was not followed up on. History being deeply disputed between the Sinhalese and Tamil ethnicities, historians of either ethnicity do not feel able to make headway in independent research. They are regularly labelled 'race traitors' or 'bigots' depending on whichever side their findings might favour. This also tends to subsume the history of Muslims, whose presence in Sri Lanka also reaches back several centuries, including in Jaffna. They have always been mainly a trading community in Sri Lanka, and then as now, the state had been wary of their economic prowess. Apparently, the eighteenth-century Dutch colonial government had sought to dismantle their economic might in Nallur and set the Tamil majority in Jaffna against them, leading to the Muslims being displaced to what is now Jaffna town, in 1728.

The location of the current Nallur Kandaswamy Temple was once a well-known Muslim settlement therefore. When Don Juan Maapana Mudaliyar built his temple in 1734, it was in close proximity to a pre-existing tomb commemorating a Sufi saint. Muslims and Hindus alike worshipped at that shrine. The temple eventually expanded to encompass this tomb as well.

According to the Muslim community in Jaffna, the temple authorities remained respectful of Muslim sentiments regarding their shrine, kept a lit lamp there in respect of the entombed saint, and gave some Muslim families exclusive camphor-selling rights around the temple in recognition of their ancestral connection to the temple grounds. This was the case till 1990 when the Muslims were evicted en masse from the area by the LTTE in pursuit of their goal of a Tamil homeland. Many Muslims have since returned to Jaffna after the civil war ended in 2009, but while they retain historical memory of the tomb and their ancestral connections to Nallur, Sufi forms of worship have been mostly erased from their current religious practices and so they no longer frequent the shrine to worship. The tomb has been walled off now and is just a memory, but scholars estimate that the Nallur phenomenon can be attributed at least in part to the existence of the tomb. While cultural memory of the phenomenon is fast fading among the current generations of Jaffna's Hindus and Muslims alike, Sufi mystics were once much revered by both communities here and their tombs were considered places of potent power and prayer fulfillment.

The Nallur phenomenon

There are hundreds of temples dotting the Jaffna peninsula now and more coming up every day. While there are a few temples that vie with Nallur for iconic status, the fact that many Tamils, not just locally, but also in the diaspora, view it as their cultural emblem to the extent of reproducing the temple and its festival in their own climes is a unique phenomenon.

Why Nallur and not any other temple? There are differing theories as to why, depending on whom you ask. Some say it is due to the historical memory of an ancient citadel of a long ago Tamil kingdom, worshiped by the kings and queens of Jaffna. It's heavily romanticised in folkloric memory therefore.

Others attribute it to the prevalence of Muruga worship in the peninsula. Jaffna's Tamils identify as mainly Saivite (worshippers of Shiva), yet worship of Murugan is much more prevalent. As in South India, he is seen as an accessible God by the masses.

Of the two temples built when the Dutch eased regulations, the first to be built was the Vannarpannai Sivan Kovil, a Shiva temple, which was much grander and ambitious in scale. It was strategically set to be the primary temple in the region. Nallur by contrast was a small temple and in the subsequent century fell afoul of the most influential Hindu revivalist of the period, Arumuga Navalar, who objected to its non-agamic style of worship including worship of the vel instead of a statue of Murugan with his co-wives.

By this time the Dutch had been driven out and the British were in power. While they were not as authoritarian as the Dutch and Portuguese colonial governments in repressing Hinduism, they had employed missionaries to convince people to convert. Many people by this time were at least nominally Christian due to centuries of enforced colonial rule, and Arumuga Navalar was working to turn back the tide. Even people nominally Hindu had apparently lost much of their understanding of the religion due to two centuries of colonial repression, and so Navalar felt the need to proselytise Hinduism to them. The folk Hinduism being practised at the time, that worshipped tridents and vels instead of statues, was not even remotely agamic, and employed practices like animal sacrifices and nautch girls. The Sivan temple being agamic did not follow these practices. Nallur Kandaswamy Temple being non-agamic did. Such practices were mocked by British and American missionaries of the time as uncouth, which enraged Navalar—so he favoured agamic Saivism which he held to be refined enough to escape missionary ridicule.

Nallur's temple authorities at the time catered to popular worship forms and wouldn't accept his position on the matter—and so for nearly his whole life of decades-long proselytisation, Navalar, despite being a resident of Nallur himself, proselytised against the Nallur Kandaswamy Temple. Despite his famed prowess as an orator though, the temple remained popular. If anything, the deeply held convictions for and against non-agamic folk religion only inflamed passions further. In time, the nautch girls and animal sacrifices did disappear. But not because Navalar said so. It is so historically distant now that many in the current generation are not even aware that this was once the case. Contemporary belief is to fast during the festival time and partake of only vegetarian food on the days of visiting the temple. It is held to be a sin to enter the temple after consuming non-vegetarian food. The only reason we even know animal sacrifices once took place at this temple's festival is because Navalar expounded on it in three long treatises. He was so enraged by it that he pursued court cases against the temple management. Sir Ponnambalam Ramanathan, his protégé and eventually, another stalwart leader of the Jaffna Tamils, joined him. The temple management won the cases. In the 1930s, yet again, a group of Brahmins tried to wrest the temple from the family that owns it, citing irregular worship and temple management. They lost too.

The modern temple

The Nallur Kandaswamy Temple is currently associated in people's minds with the history and traditions of the region, but interestingly it is also known for its modernity, creativity and trendsetting. The temple structure keeps evolving, and in doing so, flouting conventional temple architectural traditions of the region. The traditionalists grumble but there is no doubting that it captures popular imagination and fascination. Jaffna's citizenry fancy themselves traditional and conventional—and they actually are, in many respects. But they are also obsessed with keeping up with modernity. The temple taps into this dichotomous nature rather well. It harks back to an ancient temple but as a relatively new structure does not feel itself obliged to preserve its structure in perpetuity as a monument—other than the original vel which still holds pride of place despite all attempts by agamic supremacists to remove it. As such the temple keeps reinventing itself with newer structures that fascinate the people. It doesn't follow trends that other temples by and large follow in Jaffna, whether they be ancient or modern. It sets it. After griping at the vastu shastra (traditional architecture) conventions Nallur is flouting, many of the other temples then follow suit.

The current Mudalali of the temple, Kumaradas Mudaliyar, who has managed the temple for nearly sixty years, is credited with most of these innovations. According to Dr T. Sanathanan, an art academic at Jaffna University, Kumaradas Mudaliyar engaged in the same type of innovations with his temple in the north as Sri Lanka's famed architect, Geoffrey Bawa in the south of Sri Lanka; constantly breaking rules and reinventing them, redefining local architecture in the process.

Despite the cribbing of traditionalists initially, many of the innovations reflect a grandeur that the locals aspire to and has thus found much favour among them. The temple's famed 'villu mandapam'—the bow-shaped, frilled arch at its primary entrance for example, was blasted as an unorthodox innovation by vastu shastra exponents. Yet it is primarily responsible for giving the temple its unique appearance that has become emblematic to it. When the Sri Lanka Tourism Bureau started putting out postcards of Jaffna in the 1970s, it became emblematic of Jaffna too. It was unique and stood out from every other temple in the area mostly still sporting colonial European architecture. Dutch style Doric columns, Anglican church-inspired bell towers and various other colonial architectural styles still grace many of the temples in Jaffna. Nallur used to have elements of these too. It still does—instead of one bell tower however, it now sports six. As Jaffna academic and art historian P. Ahilan put it, 'The temple structure is an eclectic mix of Dravidian, Mughal and colonial European architecture.'

Alongside this, as Dr Sanathanan points out, it is also the current temple owner-cum-manager's aspirational Jaffna architecture that takes new forms not seen before. This is quickly copied by others, to become regular features of the region. Despite the temple regularly flouting conventions, much to the annoyance of stalwarts in this conventional community, it keeps growing in popularity and is seen as a major trendsetter. It appears to effectively tap into Jaffna citizens' psyche as to what they want represented before they can cognise it themselves. And then they follow suit en masse.

The temple also sports contrasts aplenty to cater to differing temperaments. From the outside, set in a sylvan setting of white sand and sturdy trees with its trademark red and white striped boundary wall, the temple has a majestic yet soothingly simple appearance. Many other temples in Jaffna by contrast are flamboyantly multicoloured. Inside the temple though, there is a lot of gilt and glamour including chandeliers on the roof catering to a unique Jaffna fascination with gilt. Even the priests doing puja carry out their traditional arathi ceremony (waving a lit lamp around the deity) with a multi-tiered candelabra of flames outshining the chandeliers above.

Timing is scrupulously observed. The temple pujas at fixed times are carried out on the dot of the specified time. In a population lackadaisical about punctuality and used to temple pujas as and when priests decide to show up, this rigid adherence to time is hugely appreciated. People from far and near know the exact time to show up for puja. Busy professionals point to this as one of the reasons they prefer to frequent this temple above others in the area. They don't need to waste their working time waiting for the puja, or show up at the appointed time only to realise that it has already taken place as the priests decided to do it early—all common issues of grouse in other temples.

Archana tickets too are still sold for Re 1—an almost meaningless amount in Sri Lanka now. This price has remained fixed for years in an apparent bid to keep it open to the masses—which the masses do indeed appreciate. While people of all castes and classes do access the temple, it isn't usual to see anyone of a too humble appearance at Nallur.

People feel obliged to deck themselves in their finest clothes when visiting Nallur. The resident deity there is known as something of a fashionista; 'Alangara Kandan' in local lingo. As one commentator put it, 'The Murugan there is "alangaram" (decked up) and so are the people visiting him.' This is not necessarily the temple management's intention, however. In recent years, they have put out rules cautioning against excessive displays of fashion as a tendency was developing for budding fashionistas to use the temple as a vantage place for flaunting their trendsetting clothing. From deliberately humble origins and wishing to retain folk elements of worship and thus accessibility to the masses—all that the vel still represents—the temple is steering new currents of elitism even as it works to keep itself accessible and relatable to everyone. The fashion scene likely sprang up thanks to its long-running festival and the tendency of people to dress in their best for it. But it was aggravated by visiting diaspora members who always put Nallur on their must-visit list when visiting home and showed up decked in their best too—sporting varying fashions from across the world. The locals not to be outdone soon started sporting outlandish fashions in the temple precincts in competition, which the temple felt a need to put a stop to. Men have to walk in shirtless and women are required to dress in culturally appropriate modest clothing. A lot of glitter can still be seen to rival the glitter of the Kandan and his palatial splendour inside, but the tendency to treat the temple as a modelling ramp has declined.

As of now, partly due to strategic leadership, partly due to historical memory and association with the old kingdom, and partly due to the popularity of Muruga worship, Nallur Kandaswamy Temple is considered foremost among the emblematic temples of Jaffna.

Sociologists and religious scholars attribute a few other reasons too for its primacy over other temples. For instance, it has the longest running festival in the country, running for twenty-five days. For well over a month including days leading up to and after the festival, hawkers set up stalls all around the temple, giving it a carnival atmosphere. In the war-torn region of Jaffna where social events are few and far between, it is a rare opportunity for families and friends to enjoy a festive atmosphere. So deeply ingrained is this cultural aspect in people's lives that diaspora Jaffna Tamils in various countries try to reproduce their own Nallur festival complete with hawkers, palmyrah products and other Jaffna regional snacks to relive their nostalgia. It is a much-awaited event in the annual calendar in Jaffna and draws not only locals, but also pilgrims and tourists from around the world including many in the diaspora who return every August to take part in the festival. All of Jaffna's hotels and numerous guest houses are full at that time. For a month, traffic has to circumnavigate a wide cut-off swathe around the temple with police posts put up to accommodate the surging crowds. Some hawkers became so popular that they became permanent businesses around the temple.

Another attributed reason is that Nallur attracted several well-known saints to its precincts. One of Jaffna's most well-known yogis of the twentieth century, Yogar Swami, his guru Chellappa Swamy, and a lady ascetic called Chadayama all preached the greatness of Lord Murugan of Nallur in its vicinity. Some of them occupied the area for years. Yogar Swamy, for example, meditated under a bilva tree near the temple for years and the crowds he drew came to associate his memory with Nallur. The temple's popularity spiked in some scholars' estimation due to the association of these venerated ascetics. Alongside this, Jaffna's well-known aesthetic exponents like Veeramani Iyer composed songs in praise of the temple that gained mass popularity—again immortalising the temple and Nallur Kandan.

In the locality, people have differing opinions—if they have an opinion at all—as to why they so revere this temple. Many are just stumped by the question. Veneration for Nallur Kandaswamy is just something that runs in their bloodstreams apparently. And so, apart from their daily or weekly visits to the temple, they will wend their way there on foot every August, decked in their best for the festival, chanting victory (arohara) to Lord Murgan by the various names (Kandan, Murugan, Vadivel, Sivabalan) he's known by: *'Kandanukku Arohara, Muruganukku Arohara, Vadivelanukku Arohara, Sivabalanukku Arohara....'*

The Nallur region becomes transformed due to their fervour, in the time of the festival. Through thick and thin, despite the vicissitudes of life visited upon them in this war-torn region, their devotion to Nallur Murugan runs deep. Long after the kings and queens who ruled alongside his reflected power are gone, he continues to rule over the people of Jaffna.

A deity for the masses. Regal and resplendent, yet also approachable and accessible. That's his draw, according to Jaffna's public. A God and his temple, emblematic of who they are, as a people.

Notes

1 There are statues of him in other parts of the temple, added later over the years. The sanctum sanctorum though holds only the vel. That's how the temple was originally built—around a vel, and now, though statues of Murugan and his wives have been added, the temple is clear that the vel will not be removed from the sanctum.

The Temples We Left Behind

Siddhartha Gigoo

A day in December 1989
Srinagar, Kashmir

Babi takes me to the shrine of Reshi Peer (the great seventeenth century saint or rishi) at Ali Kadal. Stray dogs are standing in front of the gate of the shrine. Like sentries they seem to be keeping vigil, barking at every unfamiliar passer-by. The wind, which has been frighteningly menacing the whole day, is now mute and frozen like the leafless poplars dotting the avenue leading up to the shrine complex. Inside the shrine are two other women. One is sitting in devout contemplation in front of the idol of Reshi Peer. She is mumbling a prayer; her eyes are shut. The other woman—a newly-wed—is perambulating the idol with folded hands. She's going around the idol over and over again without stopping, as if she was going away forever and never coming back. On her lips is a prayer too.

Babi says her prayers and offers a niyaz (offering) while I sit in a corner looking at a pair of wooden clogs believed to have belonged to the Rishi.

Reshi Peer's shrine has been Babi's go-to place in all circumstances. 'I am going to Reshi Peer's. Would you like to come along?' she asks me whenever she is about to go there. After all, I am her eldest grandchild—my sister is barely ten. Moreover, Babuji isn't much of a temple-goer. His laboratory—the Imperial Clinical Laboratory—is a ten-minute walk from the shrine, in Maharaj Gunj, the trader locality of Srinagar. He bicycles past the shrine twice a day, but seldom stops to go inside. Not that he's an atheist, but because he's content with his own beliefs and doesn't believe in idol worship—he's a devout Arya Samaji like his father who introduced the Arya Samaj to Kashmir.

Before leaving, the women exchange furtive glances. We are now headed home. But as we near our locality, Babi turns left into the Roopa Bhawani lane. At the end of the lane, by the banks of the Jhelum, is a small temple. Next to the temple is a small house. It is the birthplace of Roopa Bhawani, the seventeenth-century saint-poetess of Kashmir.

We are the only two people inside the temple. A portrait of Roopa Bhawani (Alakheswari) is placed inside a glass enclosure by the window. Roopa Bhawani is sitting in deep contemplation at the feet of her father and spiritual guru, Pandit Madhav Joo Dhar. Babi sits in front of the portrait and prays. Once again, she prays for continuity and fortitude. 'May the darkness dispel. May we never have to leave our beautiful house, our beautiful land! May we live and die happily here. May my children and grandchildren flourish …'

She walks around Roopa Bhawani's portrait and the Shiv Linga next to it seven times while I sit by the window looking at the Jhelum. Nawa Kadal is to the left and Safa Kadal is to the right. The Jhelum flows quietly under the two bridges that are in sight. At a distance is Hari Parbat, the abode of Mother Goddess Sharika, who, as the belief goes, granted a boon to

Madhav Joo Dhar that she would be reborn to his wife and known as Roopa Bhawani.

When we leave the temple premises, we see our cow and her calf waiting in the lane. Babi takes a piece of bread out of her bag and feeds them.

'Shall we go to the Ram Mandir?' Babi asks. 'We won't be long.'

We walk past our house towards Ram Mandir. In the summer, I would play cricket in the courtyard of the temple complex. But today, the courtyard is vacant. The priest-caretaker's quarters are locked. There is talk in Pandit households that he was forced to flee after receiving a death threat from a militant outfit.

Babi goes inside the temple while I stand by the balustrade and look at the ghat below. The majestic Hari Parbat is still in sight. Whenever you look at it, you feel comforted. But everything is bleak today. It feels as if something terrible is about to happen.

Babi comes out of the temple. Sensing my restlessness, she gives me a cheerful look. But I know what she is going to say next. We have one more temple to visit. Babi is good at coaxing people.

Janambhoomi is not a temple like other temples. A small wooden door opens up to a large compound filled with nettles and shrubs. There is an old well at the far end of the compound. We walk down a flight of stairs made of tiles and reach a basin made of stone. In summer, it brims with water. And if you are lucky, you will see goldfish. There is a Shiv Linga next to the stone idol of Lord Ram. An idol of Lord Krishna protected by small slabs of stone is a marvellous sight. Something about this place is ancient. The stone structure resembles the stone structure of the Martand Sun Temple in Mattan, Anantnag.

Everything is floundering. The houses of Pandits flanking the compound wear a sombre look. The eagle nests atop the leafless poplars are empty. Once again, I am overcome by a strange foreboding that something bad is about to happen.

Babi lights a joss stick and places it in front of the idols. A sweet fragrance fills the air. Babi mumbles the same prayer. 'May we always be happy in our homes! May our hearths be warm and well lit! May our children prosper and flourish! May Maej Kasheer (Mother Kashmir) always protect us! May this Reshevaer (Valley of Saints) thrive!'

Babi: Do you think it will snow tonight?

Me: Yes, I think it will.

Babi: You're wrong. We are a few more days away from the first snowfall of the season. You need to learn how to read the wind.

Me: When will you teach me?

Babi: When you are ready to sit in front of me.

Evening

Some of our belongings are lying next to tin trunks. Utensils … bedding. Babi is preparing for the inevitable. 'May we never be thrown out of our home,' Babi continues to mumble.

***

A day in August 1996 (six years later)

Tourist Reception Centre, Srinagar

I reach Srinagar. I have grown a beard hoping to pass off for a Muslim. Nobody except my father and mother know that I am here. I try my best to conceal my identity while asking an autorickshaw driver to take me to Downtown.

Autorickshaw driver: What are you doing here, Panditji?

Me: I came to visit my house.

He: You must go back right now or else…

Me: Will you take me to Downtown?

He: Where exactly in Downtown?

Me: Ram Mandir Lane, Safa Kadal.

He: I can't take you there. Go back to Jammu or Delhi or wherever you have come from. It is for your own good.

Me: I will, but only after seeing my house.

He: But why did you come back here?

Me: To visit my house.

He: I don't understand. You were not supposed to return. If anyone sees you in my autorickshaw, I will be in trouble. Leave now and do not come back. Don't take my refusal otherwise. I am saying this to you because I am your well-wisher.

Lal Chowk resembles a war zone. There are military bunkers all around. It seems as if a battle is about to take place. A scene from the movie, *Lion of the Desert*, which my father took me to watch in Regal cinema a few years ago, comes alive.

I have just one more hour, and then at 6 p.m., the curfew will come into effect again until tomorrow. I assess the odds of walking all the way to my old house in Safa Kadal and then getting back before the curfew. After assessing the risks, I give up.

***

A day in the spring of 1989
Home, Srinagar

It is Ram Navmi. We are preparing to go to Ram Mandir. My sister and I are wearing new clothes. Everyone is dressed up for the occasion. Like always, Pandit families from all over Kashmir will arrive here and the temple will be the centre of attraction.

Hundreds of thousands of Pandit families start arriving at Ram Mandir to take part in the festivities. By evening, they have said their prayers, and partaken of the sacred prasad—kheer, halwa and puri—served in earthen containers. We call it 'naveed'. Kids love it.

Muslims watch through the windows of their houses.

People part on a happy note. 'We will see you on Krishna Janamashtami now,' they say. Smiles reflect hope.

Janambhoomi resembles a fairground today.

***

A day in January 2018
Srinagar

I am on a visit to Srinagar. Once again, a tourist in my own land! I am accompanying a documentary film crew who are shooting a web series on the conflict in Kashmir. The film is titled *Kashmir: The Story*. After telling them everything about the place, my growing up days, and the conditions in which we were forced to flee, the crew decides to shoot in my old locality and inside the Ram Mandir complex. They want me to recount the memory of old days once again.

I walk up and down the Ram Mandir lane several times

before mustering the courage to step inside. The broken gate—a familiar vestige from the past! From outside, I can tell what awaits me. Such is the condition of the temple.

An old memory of Ram Navmi comes alive. The day the temple was decorated like a bride. The idols were decorated. The engravings in the walls and the murals cleaned and polished.

The entire courtyard now is a garbage dump. Animal droppings are all over the place. The stench is unbearable.

What was once a hallowed place of worship—the sanctum sanctorum—where the idols of our gods and goddesses were kept is now a damaged structure defaced by graffiti. The atrocious words written in English and Urdu are a telltale sign of hate and resentment towards the temple and temple-goers. Such words must not even be read or uttered. But such words, no matter how bad, must not be forgotten either, for such words changed the course of our lives.

The engravings, the ornate paintings, venerable objects of worship and symbols of our culture and heritage gone as if they had never existed! Such is the extent of defilement. It's a devastating sight. The temple narrates the account of discretion by those who deliberately wanted to erase history. It's not just an act of desecration of a temple and the temple complex. It's an act of willful obliteration of a centuries-old indigenous culture and way of life. Our way of life!

Babi's prayer—May the darkness dispel ... May we never get to leave our beautiful house, our beautiful land ... May we live and die happily here ... May we never be thrown out of our home—wraps me up yet again.

I look at the boy standing by the railing with his gaze fixed at Hari Parbat. Unlike me, he never left the place. He hid himself in the secret place near the ghat when the temple was pillaged over and over again, and when everything precious was stolen, damaged and destroyed.

As I leave the temple premises, an elderly man who has been keeping an eye on me all the while stops me and says, 'Do you think we Muslims did this? This was the army's handiwork. You must know…' He goes on and on about how the security forces were responsible for the devastation. How they occupied the temple in the '90s and turned it into a bunker.

I have neither the patience nor the time for such distortions.

The film crew sets up the shot.

'The camera will start rolling when you come out of the lane, start walking on the bridge and stop to look at the temple,' says the director.

In front of me is Ram Mandir. It has turned golden in the light of dusk. Children are laughing and making mirth. My grandmother's prayer, which I have learnt by heart, comes out and flies towards the temple.

'May you always protect us …'

Babi's dream is still alive.

***

4 a.m.
One morning in April 1990
Home, Srinagar, Kashmir

The sun is yet to rise. Father and Mother are getting my sister and me ready. A small bag is packed for us to take along. In it are a few clothes, a water bottle and a tiffin.

Our neighbours, the Koul family, are also getting ready.

The truck has arrived and is parked some fifty paces from our houses. Their house is almost empty. Everything is in the back of the truck now. Everything except the big mortar made of stone. Ratni aunty is sobbing but afraid of being heard by the Muslim neighbours. Her father-in-law, a retired police constable, is staring at his house as if it were his son about to leave for foreign shores forever.

Husband and wife start speaking in hushed tones in the verandah.

Husband: Have you taken everything?

Wife: How many times will you make me repeat?

Husband: What about the mortar? Are we going to leave it behind? Did you check the attic? What if you have forgotten some things? Go inside and check one more time. What about the kitchen?

Wife: Why can't you keep your voice low? You will wake the neighbours and land us in trouble.

Husband: Check everything again.

Wife: There is no more room in the truck. What do you want me to do? Did you lock the rooms? Lock the gate now.

The Sikh truck driver is constantly turning to his wristwatch. 'We must hurry,' he says to the family, unhappy at the delay. 'We must leave before the light breaks or else... We must cross the Jawahar tunnel in Banihal before noon... If it snows, we will get stranded...'

Mother instructs my sister never to let go of my hand. We hop into the truck.

Do we need to cover our faces? Ratni aunty asks the truck driver.

Isn't it obvious, is what the truck driver's look conveys.

Aunty: Will you please take the Ram Mandir lane while leaving?

Truck driver: It's too narrow for the truck.

Aunty: Then stop for a while when you are near the temple; I will get off and come back in a jiffy.

Aunty's daughter: Don't be mad, Ma.

Aunty: I am not mad.

Sister: Where are we going?

Aunty: Jammu.

Sister: What about Ma and Pa and Babi and Babujee?

There are no goodbyes. Everything is hush-hush and rushed.

By the time I look back, the truck has already left our home far behind and the haze has swallowed everything. I want to get off the truck and run back home. My sister has fallen asleep.

***

Evening
Jammu Bus Terminus

We have nowhere to go. There is chaos everywhere. Pandits are arriving in trucks. Hundreds of trucks are lined up along the road leading to the bus terminus. We spend the night in the truck stranded by the roadside.

The next evening, a kind soul arranges some shelter for us in a building in Talaab Tillo. 'If you choose to forgo it, some other family will take it,' he says. 'Grab the place quick or else be prepared to spend more days on the roads of Jammu.'

We are taken to a building. It is a buffalo shed that has been converted into a camp for displaced Pandits. We are shown an overcrowded dormitory in the building. Some kind people make some room for us. Ratni aunty springs into action. I start counting the people in the dormitory. I lose count at twenty-seven. My sister asks for a chilled cola.

From a cold winter dawn at home to a scorching night in the camp. It's been the longest day of my life.

There is only one question. What's going to happen now? The next morning, I hear the sound of temple bells. In front of the building is a Shiv temple. Some camp dwellers are waking their children up to take them to the temple. They continue to speak in hushed tones—fearing that their neighbours will still hear their voices. Fear didn't leave them for months.

An evening in the summer of 1990
Udhampur

The truck carrying Father, Mother, Babi and Babuji arrives. We start unloading the truck. I ask my father. What about the other things? Books, paintings, collectibles? He shakes his head.

We take up a two-room set on rent. After some days, Babi discovers a Shiv temple in the neighbourhood. Then she decides to set up a small shelf for herself. There are no idols to be placed on the shelf. Just an almanac and a portrait of some gods and goddesses!

***

Summer of 1996
Udhampur

Bedridden for months now, Babuji seems to be dreaming a happy dream. His smile says it all. The sores on his body have turned ashen—a sign that the end is near.

Babi narrates a story about our days in Khrew when we lived in grandfather's ancestral house located next to a hill atop which was the temple of Goddess Jwala (Zala). 'Do you remember teaching him how to make a slingshot?' she whispers into his ear. 'Standing beneath the vermillion-coloured rock, you taught him dangerous things like how to entice kites with the sacred offering—goat lungs. And then kites would swoop like arrows and snatch an offering from your hand.'

Babi is hopeful that her husband will die a happy death only when such stories are whispered into his ears. 'Someday, when we go back, we will start over…' she says.

***

24 June 2012
Jammu—Srinagar

Babi rings me up from Srinagar. She's on a short trip there. I coax her to go to all the places. 'Go to Reshi Peer's, Roopa Bhawani's, Ram Mandir, Durga Naag, Kheer Bhawani, Zala…' I say to her.

Babi: Will you come with me?

Me: Go to Safa Kadal too.

She: You mean to say, home?

***

Summer 2018
Home, New Delhi

My sister, Henna, is back from a trip to Srinagar. She sends me photos and videos of our old house and Ram Mandir. The graffiti, the wreckage, and the desecrated walls of the sanctum—the saddest sight! The temple of my childhood, the temple of my grandmother is still in abject condition, in a state of neglect, evoking fear and anger, waiting desperately to be restored to its old glory.

Sister: Did you see the photos and videos?

Me: Yes, all of them.

She: You saw Babi and Babuji's room... Our house... Ram Mandir...

I am sad and angry. But I try to conceal my emotions.

She: Our memories... Our childhood...

Me: Yes, but it is over.

She: Don't say that. Nothing is over. We shall go back and rebuild everything that we lost and that once was ours.

***

If you search for 'Ram Mandir, Safa Kadal, Srinagar' on Google, you will see some photos and videos of the temple as well as the condition it is in.

***

According to the survey conducted by the Kashmiri Pandit Sangharsh Samiti (KPSS), an association of Kashmiri Pandits, almost 550 temples have been desecrated, damaged and encroached upon in Kashmir between 1990 and 2020.

According to the state government, of the 438 temples in Kashmir, 208 were damaged between 1990 and 2020.

In 2019, the Government of India announced the setting up of a committee to survey and reopen around 50,000 temples that were closed in Kashmir ever since the armed insurgency erupted in 1990.

Not a single temple has been restored to its old glory.

(Excerpted from the author's memoir, titled *A Long Season of Ashes*.)

Editor

Karthik Venkatesh grew up in Bangalore, speaking Tamil, Malayalam, Kannada, English, Dakhani and Hindi. Once an MBA, he later studied education and taught English and History at a school. He has written two books for children: *10 Makers of the Indian Constitution: Stories of 10 Indians Who Shaped the Nation* and *10 Indian Languages and How They Came to Be*.

Contributors

Manu S. Pillai is the author of many books of history, including, *False Allies: India's Maharajahs in the Age of Ravi Varma, Rebel Sultans: The Deccan from Khilji to Shivaji* and *Gods, Guns & Missionaries: The Making of the Modern Hindu Identity*. His first book, *The Ivory Throne: Chronicles of the House of Travancore* (2015) won the Sahitya Akademi Yuva Puraskar.

Indira Viswanathan Peterson is Professor of Asian Studies, Emerita, Mount Holyoke College, USA. Her major publications include *Poems to Siva: The Hymns of the Tamil Saints* (1989), *Design and Rhetoric in a Sanskrit Court Epic: The Kiratarjuniya of Bharavi* (2003), and *Arjuna and the Hunter* (2016). She is co-author, with George Michell, of *The Great Temple at Thanjavur: A Thousand Years* (2010), and co-editor, with Davesh Soneji, of *Performing Pasts: Reinventing the Arts in Modern South India* (2008).

Meera Iyer is a writer and researcher. Her work focusses on helping people connect with places through history and culture. She writes on history, heritage and culture for several leading publications and dailies in India and is a columnist with *Deccan Herald*. She is the lead author of the book *Discovering Bengaluru* (2019) and the editor of *Eleven Stops to the Present: Stories of Bengaluru,* a collection of short stories for children by eleven authors (2020). She is the Convenor of INTACH Bengaluru Chapter. She has a PhD in Forest Ecology.

Basav Biradar is an independent researcher, writer, journalist and documentary filmmaker based in Bengaluru. His research interests lie at the intersection of history, culture and art. He also teaches courses on Modern Indian Theatre and Indian cinema as a visiting faculty at Azim Premji University.

Shrenik Rao is the editor-in-chief of the *Madras Courier,* a 234-year-old newspaper, now an award-winning digital publication. He is an alumnus of the London School of Economics and a (2016) Fellow at the Reuters Institute for the Study of Journalism, University of Oxford.

Siddhartha Sarma is an author and journalist. His most recent novel is *Twilight in a Knotted World,* set in Central India in the early nineteenth century.

Neelesh Kulkarni is a management graduate from Delhi University and an entrepreneur since 1985. He is also a theatre and voice-over artist, cricket commentator, public speaking coach and author. His first book (co-authored with Vikrant Pande), *In the Footsteps of Rama: Travels with the Ramayana,* was published in 2021. He has also written *Uprising: The Liberation of Dadra and Nagar Haveli*.

Vikrant Pande has to date translated twelve Marathi books into English. His book (co-authored with Neelesh Kulkarni), *In the Footsteps of Rama: Travels with the Ramayana,* published in 2021, was a bestseller. Vikrant's translation of Girish Kuber's Marathi work, *Tatayan, The Tatas: How a Family Built a Business and a Nation* won the Gaja Capital Best Business Book Award of 2019. Vikrant is a graduate of IIM Bangalore.

Trisha Gupta is an independent writer and critic based in Delhi, and an Associate Professor at the Jindal School of Journalism and Communication. She studied history at Delhi University and anthropology at the University of Cambridge and Columbia University. Since 2007, she has written on literary and cultural subjects for a wide range of Indian publications, including a weekly column on cinema for the *Mumbai Mirror* (now *TOI Plus*) for seven years. Her published writing is archived on her blog *Chhotahazri*—www.trishagupta.blogspot.com.

Haroon Khalid is an author and a freelance journalist, who has written five books and over 350 articles. In his work, Haroon explores fluid identities, traditions and religious practices that challenge the notion of exclusivist identities that define communities in South Asia today. He has an academic background in anthropology and is currently based in Canada.

Amish Raj Mulmi is the author of *All Roads Lead North: Nepal's Turn to China* (Context, 2021). His writings have appeared in *Al Jazeera, Roads and Kingdoms, Himal Southasian,* and *The Kathmandu Post* among others. He is consulting editor at Writer's Side Literary Agency.

Thulasi Muttulingam is a journalist based in Jaffna, Sri Lanka. She primarily focuses on long form journalism tracking social issues prevailing in post war Sri Lanka. She also likes to research on the whys and wherefores of social phenomena in the region.

Siddhartha Gigoo is a Commonwealth Prize-winning author. In 2015, he won the Commonwealth Short Story Prize (Asia) for his short story, *The Umbrella Man*. He has written two books of poetry, four novels—*The Garden of Solitude, Mehr: A Love Story, The Lion of Kashmir,* and *Love in the Time of Quarantine*—and a book of short stories—*A Fistful of Earth and Other Stories* (longlisted for the Frank O'Connor International Short Story Award 2015). He has also co-edited two anthologies, namely *A Long Dream of Home: The Persecution, Exodus and Exile of Kashmiri Pandits* and *Once We Had Everything: Literature in Exile.* His short stories have been longlisted for the Lorian Hemingway Short Story Prize, Royal Society of Literature's V.S. Pritchett Short Story Prize, and Seán O' Faoláin Short Story Prize. Siddhartha's short films, *The Last Day* and *Goodbye, Mayfly,* have won several awards at international film festivals. His writings appear in various literary journals.